THE VOYAGE OF A
SHEPHERD BOY

THE VOYAGE OF A SHEPHERD BOY

PANAGIOTIS N. SYMBAS

Copyright © 2009 by Panagiotis N. Symbas.

Library of Congress Control Number: 2009907301
ISBN: Hardcover 978-1-4415-5742-1
Softcover 978-1-4415-5741-4

All rights reserved. No part of this book may be reproduced or transmitted in any form or by any means, electronic or mechanical, including photocopying, recording, or by any information storage and retrieval system, without permission in writing from the copyright owner.

This book was printed in the United States of America.

To order additional copies of this book, contact:
Xlibris Corporation
1-888-795-4274
www.Xlibris.com
Orders@Xlibris.com
66181

CONTENTS

INTRODUCTION 9

PART A

I. OUR VILLAGE 13
II. OUR FAMILY 17
III. LIFE IN THE VILLAGE 22
IV. HIGH SCHOOL YEARS 36
    1. SECOND WORLD WAR 43
    2. UPRISING AGAINST THE OCCUPYING FORCES 48
    3. FIRST PRISON CAMP 59
    4. CIVIL WAR 67
V. FIRST STEP TOWARDS HIGHER EDUCATION 80
    1. ARMED FORCES SERVICE 84
    2. SECOND PRISON CAMP 87
    3. RETURN TO MY VILLAGE 101
VI. UNIVERSITY YEARS 103

PART B

VII. INTRODUCTION TO MY NEW COUNTRY 125
VIII. THE MAKING OF A CARDIOTHORACIC SURGEON 133
IX. POLISHING THE CARDIAC SURGEON 153
X. ACADEMIC LIFE 157
    1. TEACHING THE STUDENTS 160
    2. TEACHING THE RESIDENTS 161
    3. RESEARCH 164
    4. ADMINISTRATIVE DUTIES 167
    5. PATIENT CARE 168

PART C

REFERENCES 185
APPENDIX—CURRICULUM VITAE 187

Dedicated to those who gave me a helping hand, especially to my wonderful sons, Drs. Nikolas, Peter and John, and my lovely wife for their love, understanding, and support during this long trip.

INTRODUCTION

Over the years during discussions with my family, I mentioned various events of my life to emphasize some facts of life in a historical perspective. Although my sons, during their tender ages, disregarded my comments, later on each one of them on many occasions suggested, and sometimes insisted that I should record my past. However, each time they asked I ignored their comments in order either to write another scientific paper or book, or to devote my available free time to review medical literature, or to spend some time with my family. Now that my remaining years are becoming shorter and shorter, I thought it might be the time to write my story. I will do it first, for the benefit of my children and, grandchildren, and second, for my own benefit, since reminiscing over even the most difficult events of my life is as invigorating now as it was then when I overcame so many obstacles. Also, there are many beautiful and happy memories that I want my wife and my sons to understand, as well as how the struggles of life made me the man that I am. Unfortunately, I have not kept a diary and as a result whatever I write is only from my own recollections. Thus, my biography is subject to the limitations of my memory. However, since my memory on medical subjects and my surgical dexterity as yet have not failed me, as is evident by the fact that Emory School of Medicine is still allowing me to teach and practice, I am confident that the events that I am about to describe are fairly accurate.

PANAGIOTIS N. SYMBAS

This text encompasses some of the events, which had a great impact in my life. My wish is that it might convince my children, grandchildren and anyone else who might read it that their dreams, with hard work and determination, are realizable no matter how unrealistic they might seem.

So, as Benjamin Franklin wrote, "I shall indulge the inclination so natural in old men, to be talking of themselves and their own past actions, and I shall indulge it without being troublesome to others who thro' respect to age might think themselves oblig'd to give me a hearing, since this may be read or not as anyone pleases."[1]

PART A

"The web of our life is a mingled yarn, good and ill together."

—William Shakespeare—

I. OUR VILLAGE

**Figure 1
Our village before its total destruction during the
Civil War.**

In 1925, I was born in a village called Dendrochori, a very picturesque village that was located in the most northwestern corner of Greece, about 20 kilometers from the Albanian and 60 kilometers from the Yugoslavian borders. There, the mountain Malimadi, which is a westward continuation of the mountain Vitsi meets the Mountain of Gramos, which is the northward continuation of the mountains Olympos and Pindos. There at the foot of the mountain Malimadi the village of Dendrohori had its two-story houses spread in a semicircular manner (Figure 1). They were built with gray limestones, which are in abundance in the mountains and they were quite close to each other and some of them were even attached to each other. All of the homes had a small yard in front or in the back, surrounded by a 5 to 8 feet tall stonewall. A thick wooden door of equal height to the walls protected the entrance to the yard. The roof of the houses was covered with red clay shingles and some of the houses were painted with white or colorful wash, and others only had painted windows. All of the homes were facing south, southeast or southwest looking towards the hilly plain, which extends for miles from the foot of the mountain to the flat land of the valley of Messopotamia. Almost all the hills of the plain, which were divided in square or rectangular pieces, were well cultivated. Some of the southwestern ones were planted with grape vines but all the rest were planted with wheat, barley, or corn. Looking from above during springtime all the hills appeared as dark green squares surrounded on the south and southeastern side by the open horizon and by the high gray mountain ridges on the north and northwestern side. The mountains below the tree line were covered with dark green oak trees and or with light green walnut trees.

From December through April the peaks of the mountains were covered with snow whereas during the rest of the year they appeared gray, the color of the limestones, which covered them. Etched in my memory, the village was a beautiful sight to see, with the changing of the season. Since most of our work was either agricultural or dealing with livestock we usually lived outdoors, and marveled at the sights, sounds and even smells of our surroundings.

As I stated earlier the name of my village was Dendrochi, the Village of Trees, from Dendro, which means tree, and Horio, which means village. Legend has it that it was established in the 15th century and that the initial inhabitants came from three other villages, which were located in lower lands. There the villagers

THE VOYAGE OF A SHEPHERD BOY

were accessible to the Turkish forces, which occupied Greece and they were subject to constant harassment and persecution. In order to minimize or avoid the constant Turkish mistreatment, the villagers established our village at the foot of the mountains. There from north, northwest and northeast, the mountains protected them, and from the south the valley was wide open providing broad visibility.

It has been said that initially the village consisted of 13 families, 100 years later it grew to 129 families, and during 1940 the population count was about 700 inhabitants. As I mentioned before the main source of survival was farming and livestock. Each family had either small or large pieces of cultivated land from which they were able to provide for their needs and some of them made enough to sell. Also, almost every family had a cow, a pig, a few goats and sheep, which provided them with wool, meat, milk, and milk products. Several families had large stocks of goats and sheep, which they used not only for their needs but also for sale. In addition, from 1917 to 1947 many of the families derived income from abroad generated by members of their families who worked elsewhere, particularly in the United States of America. All in all, the families in the village supported and cared for each other. The villagers as a rule were frugal and hard working, competitive and proud as well as resourceful, and progressive. These traits coupled with their available sources for living made the people more or less self-sufficient. As a result, during the Second World War when the Greek population as a whole was deprived not only of its freedom but also from everything else including the essentials for survival, the people in this remote corner of Greece had enough to sustain themselves and nobody died of starvation. Unfortunately, this was not true for the rest of my native country, especially for the people in the major cities where hundreds of thousand perished from starvation.

From the last part of December through the first part of March almost all of the land was covered with snow. At night, during those months all family members and friends would gather at home around the flickering light of a kerosene lamp, and around the wood-burning stove or fireplace, talking, singing, or pursuing their own interest; such as reading, needling, sewing, etc. During the day most men spent their time in a café sipping Greek coffee, playing cards, reading newspapers, and debating various issues. A few men, those who had large herds of goats or sheep would be out at the barns taking care of them. Women as a rule stayed home taking care of the house and during their free time they would meet with friends for coffee or tea. All the children were at school Monday through Friday from 8 o'clock to 12 noon and from 1 o'clock to 5 o'clock pm, and also Saturday from 8 o'clock to 12 noon.

During the rest of the year all able adults were outdoors working, plowing, seeding, harvesting, gardening, etc. At night most of them returned home to have supper and rest while the village was deadly quiet, covered in darkness or sometimes with golden moonlight. Only the dogs' barking, the owls' singing, the goats' bellows frequently interrupted the silence. At dawn bursting noise spread all over the village and each of the villagers like honeybees were hurrying out of the village to whatever work they had to do that day.

Before the various civil disobediences and especially before the Communist war, everybody was working harmoniously for the individual good and for the common good. During this time the village prospered and thrived. Unfortunately, however, this harmony and common support lasted only until 1942. Then after external political and ideological differences were introduced into the life of the villagers, especially during the war against the communist which resulted not only in the loss of harmony and support for each other but also in the total loss of trust between each other and even between close relatives. This atmosphere continued until the total physical destruction of the village in 1947, and the dispersion of the villagers to all corners of the world and especially behind the Iron Curtain.

II. OUR FAMILY

I am the youngest of five siblings, born on August 15 1925. Our immediate family consisted of my father, Nikolaos T. Symbas, my mother, Eleni Tsemanis Symbas, my brother, Naum Nikolaos Symbas, my sister Vasiliki Symbas Noliou, my brother John Nikolaos Symbas, my sister Ioanna Symbas Angelkos, and Me Panagiotis Nikolaos Symbas. My father passed away at the age 83, my mother at age of 100, my brother Naum at the age of 85, and my sister Vasiliki at the age of 89. My brother John, age 86, and my sister Ioanna, age 84 years old are still living.

My father was stern, rather harsh, fearless, and strong, both physically and mentally. He vigorously supported what he felt was right and he always spoke his mind no matter what the consequences might be. This characteristic almost cost him his life during the communist Gorilla war in the forties. He spent all his life in our village except for two occasions for a period of 2 and 9 years respectfully when he came willingly to America to work and then on one occasion for 10 years, when by force he was taken by the Communists with my mother and my sister Vasiliki to Poland at the end of the Civil War in 1947.

In contrast to my father, my mother was thin, of medium statue, extremely gentle, and loved by everyone, she was the consummate lady. She always approached everything in a calm and loving way and never spoke adversely about anyone. Characteristically, she used to say, "If you do not have anything good to say about someone, do not say anything". She was born in a prominent family of our village, but unfortunately, at the age of 6 she lost her father. He was apparently murdered by a group of Bulgarian sympathizers. Following his death both of her brothers left for America. As a result of these unfortunate events and the overall turmoil that our part of Greece was experiencing then, she was unable to attend school. She married my father at the age of 16 years. Despite her lack of formal education, she was a consultant and advisor on every issue not only to us but also to all her friends and relatives. She was indeed, gentle, unconditionally loving and certainly a wise lady too.

My oldest brother Naum was a very handsome man with curly blond hair and green eyes. He was a prestigious tailor in our village. He was also very sociable, a good dancer, and singer and always the central figure in any social group. Unfortunately, due to the fact that he was 17 years my senior, and due to my departure from the village at a very young age, I did not have the opportunity to become close to him. In addition during my early childhood he married and established his own household (Figure 2). As a result, I remember him as a father figure and an advocate for my advanced education.

**Figure 2
Picture at my brother Naum's wedding. Me
sitting in front
of the bride and my father.**

THE VOYAGE OF A SHEPHERD BOY

My oldest sister Vasiliki was a gentle, kind lady that kept a low profile. She was 15 years older than I was. She married to Manolis Nolis and moved out of our house when I was just a young boy. As a result, I got to know her only much later in the course of our lives. Before World War II her husband migrated to Australia to gain opportunities and provide better support for his family. As a result, she was left alone to take care of their three daughters as well as her mother-in-law and sister-in-law. In order to make this heavy burden easier on many occasions we worked together in the fields especially during the War against the communist. She was a kind, stoic, hardworking lady who never complained about the adversities that she faced. She was the pillar of her family for about 12 years until she was taken by the communist to Poland and from there managed to join her family in Australia.

My brother John although only 4 years older than me, has always stood as my strongest protector and advocate, as he was for the rest of our family. He supported us all unconditionally. Although I could describe numerous occasions in my life where he showed his selfless support for me, the most auspicious one was when we were released from the army and we were at a great crossroad in our lives. At that time the only thing that we possessed was the army uniform that we wore. Our parents had been taken by force behind the Iron Curtain and our property was burned and destroyed during the war against the Communist. We only had each other. As a result, I was planning to first find a job in order to secure some funds for survival, and then to start thinking about my studies. However, while discussing this issue and other concerns with him he in his own characteristically categorical way stated, "No, you are going to immediately begin your studies and together as we go along we will find solutions for all our challenges". He then gave me a few drachmas that he had saved from his own labor and bade me farewell. This wonderful gesture, the unconditional support, was what I needed to start my challenging road ahead. John is a man of iron will, extremely stoic, hardworking, frugal, selfless, and a strong supporter of what is good for everyone in the family no matter what the cost to himself. John has been an exemplary brother and a superb friend.

Finally comes my sister Anna who, although only two years older than me, was my baby sitter when my mother and the rest of our family had to work in the fields. However, when we were left alone she was afraid more than I was and yet she always stood by me until nightfall when everyone returned from the fields. Since that time she has continued to stand by me whenever I needed her. She is kind, compassionate, hardworking, and completely dedicated to her family especially to her two daughters. All of her life she has shown great strength working outside of the home as hard as anyone and afterward taking care of the other entire household needs as well. During my teens she married Stavro Angelkos and they began their separate family.

Nevertheless no matter how much each member of our family was dedicated to each other this did not mean that we were always working in absolute harmony. Considering the individuality and the strong will of each one of us, and in some cases absolute stubbornness, we had our share of disagreements, arguments, and even fighting. However, whatever our differences and conflicts were, we would resolve them quickly and proceed with our normal lives on loving terms.

According to the standards of living then, our family was considered affluent. This was due to the fact that we had large herds of livestock, and a considerable farmland, with a significant portion of it irrigatable. We produced almost everything that we needed and more, wheat, corn, barley, milk, milk products, wool, vegetables, and fruit. We had an abundance of wood for burning, building, and for furniture. As a result, we were more or less self-sufficient. All our food was homemade from our produce, and our clothing and our blankets were made from our wool and even our working shoes were homemade from the skin of our animals.

This state of well-being and self-sufficiency, however, came at a significant price. All the male members of the family, rain

THE VOYAGE OF A SHEPHERD BOY

or shine, winter or summer, were constantly outdoors working very hard. During the wintertime we would feed and take care of the livestock and during the summer in addition we would work in the fields.

Also, all female members of the family were also working constantly. During the winter they would make fabric and blankets, knit sweaters, socks, and gloves from wool, bake our bread to feed our employees and us as well as take care of many other household needs. During the summer they too would work in the fields with the men, gathering and harvesting and transporting all the valuable crops.

III. LIFE IN THE VILLAGE

Every child under 12 years old, in our village was required to attend school and graduate from middle school. In Greece even then this was demanded and enforced by the government. The time required for schooling was 7 years, one year for kindergarten and 6 years to complete lower and middle school. During the school year period from October to June no child was permitted to be occupied by any other chore or stay idle. School was mandatory.

Our school was located in the center of our village close to our church and to one of the two squares. It was a two level structure built from lime stones. The ground floor had a large hall, which was used by the students when not in class and when the weather was bad. In addition there was one classroom for the kindergarten and a couple of storage rooms. In the center of the next floor there was a square hall surrounded by three classrooms and one office room. All of the rooms had high ceilings and larger windows facing either the mountains or the open hilly valley. In each classroom there was a blackboard. Facing it there were two rows of four or five benches long enough for three or four students to sit on each one of them. On the sides and between the two rows of benches there was a passage wide enough for one individual to pass through. On one side of the blackboard facing the benches there was a desk and a chair for the teacher and on the other side a stove for heating the class from November to March. The boys were sitting on one side and the girls on the other in sequential order, the short in front and the tall in the back.

Classes began at 8:00 a.m. and continued until noon when everybody walked home to have lunch. At 1:00 p.m. everybody except the kindergarten students returned to classes until 5:00 p.m. This schedule was from Monday to Friday. Whereas on Saturday the classes were held only from 8:00 a.m. to noontime. Each one of these sessions consisted of a fifty-minute class work period and a ten-minute rest period. The dress code for boys was short pants just above the knees; long socks up to the knees and hair cut flush to the skull. For girls a long dress was required that hit just below the knees and long socks up to the knees.

From November to March when heating the classroom was necessary, each student was expected to carry to school in addition to his books, a piece of wood for the stove. During winter most of the time there was snow on the ground reaching sometimes up to 50 cm. Walking from home to school through the snow, my bare knees and my whole body shivered. Upon arriving in the classroom with the wooden stove in full blast I thought I had arrived at an oasis.

Every morning just before classes began no student was allowed to enter the classrooms, unless the weather was extremely bad. Everyone waited in the schoolyard either reviewing his or her schoolwork for the day or playing together. The older boys in addition were very discreetly flirting with the girls until the school bell rang, signaling the time to begin classes. All the students ran into the classrooms, which were abuzz with children's voices. This pleasant noise lasted until the teacher appeared in the door when everybody jumped in attention and a dead silence spread throughout the room. While we stood one student, or sometimes the entire class invoked the "Lord's Prayer", and then everybody took his or her seat. First we turned in our written homework and next we were randomly tested orally on the assigned subject. It was of interest that the teacher would usually pick students who were unprepared, I guess by observing who was avoiding eye contact with him or who perhaps was hiding behind his classmate. After this feared and dreaded ritual for some of the students, and entertaining for others, the teacher would proceed with the presentation of the new material. In order to keep our attention during the presentation unexpectedly, we would be asked to repeat what the teacher just said. We were expected to know all the subjects which were assigned to us, and to have completed all the homework. Unexcused failure to do so was always accompanied with some form of punishment. The penalty varied from staying after school to finish the work, to reporting our delinquency to our parents, which of course was always accompanied with some form of punishment at home.

In addition to the academic expectations, special behavior was expected from all the students i.e. respect for school and other property, respect for classmates, and all villagers, and especially respect for teachers. Violation of this code of conduct was accompanied with punishment from the teachers and the parents, which sometimes was of a corporal nature.

During my school years we had four teachers for about 100 students, one of them taught kindergarten and the other three taught two classes each. One teacher taught the first and second grades, the third and fourth grades were taught by another, while the senior teacher taught the fifth and sixth grades. Our teachers were the most respected citizens among the adult villagers, and the people that were most respected and feared by the students. Except the kindergarten teacher, the other schoolteachers were from other parts of Greece.

Nevertheless they were incorporated among us and considered part of our small community.

When I started kindergarten I was terribly frightened, as I presume everyone was. The anxiety of facing the unknown and the uncertainty of meeting the expectations of my family and teachers was daunting. As time went on however, not only did these fears vanish but I also found myself unexpectedly at the center of attention in my class. Perhaps this was due to the

THE VOYAGE OF A SHEPHERD BOY

fact that I was doing well, something that I do not remember, or because as I was told later, my teacher was in love with my older brother Naum. My first grade teacher was a nice but totally un-inspiring lady. Despite this shortcoming however, I continued to enjoy school. None of the members of my family were directly pushing me to do well, nor have they ever throughout all my school years. Their hidden desire for me to excel, and their praises were sufficient to keep me focused in my schoolwork.

Beginning in my third grade, a new teacher, Lazaros Hatjizisis was transferred to our village. He was very young, about the age of my oldest brother Naum. He was a very vivacious man, enthusiastic in his teaching, which he obviously enjoyed. He was a disciplinarian but pleasant in his relationship with the villagers and also with his students. Out of the class he enthusiastically participated in some of our games and in other extracurricular activities. Even during these activities, however, he continued to encourage us to do well, to teach us discipline and teamwork, and to expect the best possible effort.

In the classroom he altered the previous formula for teaching, and brought in additional teaching material not required by the national department of education, with the financial help from some of the parents. This change as will be mentioned later helped me greatly during the entrance examination for high school. This new teacher taught us zealously, giving one hundred percent of his energy and in return, he was expecting equal commitment on our part. His teaching style was pleasant, even humorous at times, but he never failed to command full attention from his students.

Fortunately for me, he was assigned to teach the third grade, which was my class as well as the fourth grade. The new atmosphere that he brought to our class increased my interest in my schoolwork and my desire to excel.

On our regular school days, I was usually awakened by my mother at seven o' clock in the morning. Because we had no running water at home a shower was feasible only once a week. So we washed our face and hands, had a quick breakfast which consisted of a slice of cheese and bread warmed or roasted in the fire or on the stove and with the books in hand we walked or ran to school.

If I arrived early for classes I either played in the schoolyard, socialized or reviewed a mathematical problem included in the day's homework with some of my classmates.

In my class, perhaps because it was perceived that I had always done my homework, I was examined on the assigned material only if my classmates failed to answer correctly. In reality, this perception was usually correct. No matter what, I always tried to be well prepared. I had a strong desire to do well, which was due in part to my desire not to fail my parents and teacher's expectations. I was frequently asked to summarize the new material that the teachers had taught us that day perhaps because they assumed that I paid close attention and that I had a good memory.

At the end of my classes, I immediately would drop my books at home and grab a piece of bread and cheese and run outside while I was devouring my snack. It was during this downtime that I relaxed and had some fun. I either played with my friends in the school or churchyard or ran outside of the village with or without some of them. Occasionally I would go with some of them or alone to the mountains or the fields to chase birds or to eat fresh fruit, apples, pears, grapes, or nuts, which were in abundance. Whatever was in season we picked either from our own trees or from someone else's trees. In the mountains I usually climbed up half the way to the summit, hopping from stone to stone, whistling, singing, and again searching for wild fruits, berries, and nuts. There in the midst of the wild flowers' aroma during spring or summer, looking down toward the village and the hilly valley I found oasis, a place for meditation. Then and there it was the time and a place for me to release all my restrained physical energy to vent the frustrations of the day, to fill my lungs with aromatic clean air and to meditate. There, surrounded by the oak trees I enjoyed the present and wondered about my future.

THE VOYAGE OF A SHEPHERD BOY

After venturing to the mountains or playing in the schoolyard for various periods of time I would return home. While supper was prepared I strove to complete my homework before we ate. Supper was our formal meal. It was served after all the members of the family who were in the village were at the table. The rest of the meals, due to the demands of the daily work were served on an individual basis. After supper I either continued my homework while the rest of my family carried out various chores in silence, or we all joined in discussions of various topics or we sang various popular melodies.

For me and most of the children, the most pleasantly anticipated days were the weekends and holidays. This was because during those days we usually had special meals and plenty of time for leisure without worries about school. During those days, my greatest desire was to spend my time at the farmhouse and barnyards particularly when our livestock was there.

Our fields were spread throughout the territory of the village, but most of the productive and irrigated ones were about 8 miles away from the village. There we had our farmhouse, hay barns, and sheep holds. They were situated on the West Bank of a tributary to the river Aliakmon surrounded by hills and mountains. On the northwestern side and behind our holdings was the mountain Malimadi rising about 1,500 meters. In front of the barns and next to the river were our fields and at a distance to the northeast stood the Mountain Vitsi.

The farmhouse was built from limestones. Its ground floor was used to house our working animals, mules, and bulls. The first floor was partitioned into two spaces. One was used to nurse any sick or weak goat or sheep, and the other, which had a fireplace, was our sleeping quarters. On either side of the fireplace we had a foot high bench. Our beds were made with straw-filled mattresses and had wool homemade blankets. On the walls there were drawers and shelves to store our food.

From the age of eight and until I finished middle school I frequently left the village for the farmhouse on Saturday after dismissal from school. I walked the eastward dirt road for about an hour and a half, passing hill after hill. I was hopping from stone to stone and sometimes running with unrestrained energy filled with overwhelming joy. I was joyful because I was temporarily away from the daily worries at home and competition at school and also because of my anticipation to see the flock of sheep and goats and our two dogs as they were approaching the barns for the night. When I was all alone I also felt a little anxious. Sometimes depending upon the season or the time of the day the road and the fields were completely deserted. Other times a few of villagers were present either returning home, or some were still in the fields carrying on their daily work.

During late autumn days I could hear the bells of some livestock and the barking of the dogs or I could see among the multicolored trees, sheep and goats, full of vigor running by and competing while picking up ripened fruit that had fallen to the ground from oaks and pear trees. In the winter the mountains stood still and quiet because the ground was frequently covered with snow. The road then was only a narrow path just enough for a mule to pass. While walking I could hear the crackle or the splash of the snow under my feet and at times the dogs barking and the wolves growling. Although my surroundings were beautiful and peaceful they were also sometimes eerie and even frightening, especially when I was walking at dusk and I heard the wolves growling. During the spring and summer seasons my walk was almost always pleasant. The road was never deserted. Someone was always coming or going to the fields and the whole atmosphere was full of vitality and noise. Every able body was working in the fields and all the village's livestock was out in the mountains or fields.

Once I reached the last major hill and I could see our farmland at a distance I felt immediate happiness. Its surrounding hills and mountains with their trees and bushes in brilliant, multicolored, red, yellow and green during autumn, dormant and overpowered during winter and lush green interspersed with multicolored flowers during spring made my heart sing. The tall poplar trees were lined up like soldiers along the banks of the river as though they were guarding the fields from the rippling or raging waters of the river. The wheat fields were lush green during early spring, waving golden brown during late spring and early summer, and dark brown in autumn after seeding. The cornfields were dense dark green while the vegetable garden was full of various shades of green crisscrossed with lines of various brightly colored flowers. No matter what season it was, the whole atmosphere as seen through the eyes of my childhood, was always pleasant and uplifting, even when set against a harsh winter.

As soon as I arrived at the farmhouse, I dropped whatever I was carrying from the village and I began hiking towards the flock. At a distance up at the mountainside I could see our black, white, or brown sheep and goats descending in a semicircular fashion. As I began approaching them our dogs sensed that somebody was coming near their precious flock, and they immediately dashed angrily towards me to prevent me from coming closer. As soon as they came close enough to determine that I was a friend, they ran gleefully towards me. Depending upon the season, the flock consisted only of the adults or both adults and youngsters. Accompanied by the shepherd, they descended down the mountain and during winter, the flock was housed in the sheep hold built of limestone walls with a wheat straw roof, where as during autumn, spring and summer the flocks were kept outdoors in the fields, or the mountains.

Then the shepherd, I and whoever else was there would settle in our cabin or in the open field next to our flock. The nights could be crispy clear with bright moon shining everywhere creating various shapes and shadows from the trees or bushes, giving me the impression that something or someone was out there, or they could be so dark as to make it impossible to see beyond a few steps. The winter nights brought a bone-chilling cold, while the autumn and spring nights were relatively comfortable. The roaring fire in the cabin's fireplace or in the open field coupled with the woolen clothes, blankets, and the special shepherd overcoats kept us relatively comfortable. The rain and cold however could sometimes be almost unbearable.

After the flock settled down everything around us was silent. The deadly silence was interrupted periodically by the dog's bark, by the sound of the goat's bells, or even by the howling of the wolves. The surroundings were at once peaceful as well as intimidating. At dawn, the frequency and the intensity of the bell sounds increased and now the bleats of the baby lamb, goats, and of their mothers looking for each other began to fill the air.

After milking the goats and sheep, the gate of the stockyard would open and all the livestock except for the youngsters were led into the mountains for grazing. When the ground was deeply covered with snow they were led outside the hayloft to be fed with hay and dry oak leaves.

After the flock moved out and before I left for the village I would go back to the pen where the baby goats and lambs were kept. As soon as I walked in, they will initially burst into running and jumping, and then they would stop, facing me with their beautiful white, black, or brown faces, as if they were wondering who this stranger is, and then they would either come to me or start jumping and running again. During early spring when the wheat was in full growth I would let them out and lead them to the wheat fields for a small taste of the fresh plants. Their beautiful clean multicolor coats against the fresh green wheat were the most vivid pictures of the beautiful spring season.

After I drew as much pleasure as I could from my visit, I departed early enough so that I could arrive in my village during daylight, and early enough to finish my next school day's homework.

The only time when my visit to our farm was sorrowful was on Holy Thursday just before Easter. That was the usual fateful day when the butchers would come from the city to purchase the male baby lambs and kids. They were led into the lush green lawn in front of the stockyard, frightened and bleating as if they knew their fate. After reaching an agreement as to the purchase price, the butchers and my father would slaughter them one after the other by slashing their throats, and splashing their innocent blood all over the fresh green grass. By afternoon their tender corpses were loaded onto a truck departing for the big city to provide the citizens there with pleasurable, delicious Easter meals.

Although, I was sad and resentful for their slaughter still at that early age, I realized the harsh reality of their destiny. This was the purpose for which they were so carefully nourished and raised.

During my leisure time, whether it was in the fields, the mountains or at home, I was glad to be away from my school, although I could not totally detach myself from it. I would always devote some time to my books, or to mentally reflect on what I was taught the previous days and weeks. Also not infrequently, particularly when I was alone up in the mountains or the open fields I would wonder whether I would like to live the type of life that my parents had or completely divert from it. Strangely, although I felt comfortable in the familiar stable environment that my parents and I were living, still I had a great desire to break away to something else. But what? My passion and path in life was initially paved by comments from my teachers and fellow villagers who advised that I should continue my pursuit of knowledge since it was said that I was passionate and talented in this regard. These suggestions gave me the outlet that I was seeking, but burdened me with bigger questions. How could this be accomplished since no one from my family had made such a venture? Only four or five people in the history of our village pursued higher education and only half of them did it successfully. Could I live up to the academic demands? How could I survive in the city alone? However, the prospect of experiencing something different abolished all these fears and inspired me to hope for a better future.

My primary school years passed one after another with the same engagements, the same thoughts and desires, and the same teachers' comments as to my future. Yet after graduation no sign was given to me as far as preparation for the high school entrance examinations. In those days in order to gain entrance into high school, the applicant had to pass the required examination on the subjects taught in the last two years of primary school. The examination was given about three months after graduation.

The candidates for high school were already preparing for it on their own or the majority, by tutoring.

My father was proud of my academic performance as well as the suggestions of my teachers and brothers to go to high school. However, he was reluctant to send me. His fear of being unable to financially support me during my high school years and potentially for an even higher education prevented him from taking such a step. So while I anxiously waited to be allowed to go to the city and take the required examination the day for it approached without anybody telling me what I need to do. Finally, a few days before the examinations I got the courage to ask my mother about it. In her usual soft and somewhat disappointed voice she said that my father could not make such a decision for financial reasons.

The thought of going to high school always evoked many different thoughts and emotions. Optimism and happiness because I would leave my environment, which I frequently considered unsuited to my dreams and to my future. I also felt anxiety, fear, and uncertainty because I had to live alone in the city away from my secured environment at only 12 years of age. I was also unsure that I would be able to successfully meet the challenges of high school.

As a result, that day when my mother indicated that I would not be able to follow my hidden dream, although I felt devastated somehow I also felt a small amount of relief. The heavy load of responsibilities that I would have to carry if I were going away momentarily was lifted. Yet the thought that I was staying in the village brought on a kind of desperation. On the one hand I lost my dream, and, on the other, I felt that physically and psychologically I was not ready and able to independently assume the responsibility of carrying on the hard labor that my

THE VOYAGE OF A SHEPHERD BOY

father and brother John were performing. In addition, I found it unacceptable to stay idle. My family sensed the desperation.

In addition, they knew that at my age I was not able to engage alone in meaningful work in the fields or in carrying for our livestock. So, in order to occupy me during the late fall, I was assigned to help my brother Naum in his tailoring shop and occasionally to assist my father and brother John in their daily work.

My daily work, except of Sundays was to open my brother Naum's shop and start the fire in the wood stove. After my brother's arrival and during the day I kept the wood charcoal iron hot and I ironed the clothes that my brother was tailoring, did some stitching and took care of other small insignificant chores.

The misty, cloudy, rainy days of late autumn and the cold heavy snow days of winter were clearly expressing my gloomy feelings. Looking outside through the windows of my brother's shop I could see no other path to follow but the footsteps of everybody else in the village. Despite this feeling of pessimism at night and whenever I was not occupied by other duties, I would always take refuge in studying my last two school year books hoping that staying close to the material in them might one day be of help.

As time passed my family noticed my unhappiness. Because of my feelings and the continued comments of my teachers and others that I was wasted with what I was doing, by mid January a decision was made by my family to attend, for no credits, the senior classes of our village school. This decision was prompted to either pacify me or to bide time until they could conclusively decide what my future would be. I was somewhat embarrassed and reluctant because I would be attending classes with schoolmates who were junior to me. However, I was also hoping that this step might mean that there was a possibility that I might be allowed to go to high school the next academic year.

Two months passed uneventfully, sometimes helping my brother Naum and the rest of the time attending classes. Unfortunately, by April when the workload for my father and brother John increased, I was delegated to help them exclusively. So from then on I spent almost all of my time away from the village on the farm, the fields or the mountains. I helped our shepherd with the adult livestock, and my father and brother in plowing and seeding the fields with the summer crop of oats and corn, etc. (Figure 3). In addition I guarded and led to grazing the young lambs and goats, which were now separated from their mothers.

**Figure 3
The shepherd boy standing in the far back and
my father with his baldhead standing in front
next to the two shepherds.**

During those months everybody's schedule was very busy if not hectic. The work began at dawn and continued until dusk and beyond. With this pace of life and work my school issue seemed to have been forgotten. Day after day I was anxiously waiting for someone from my family to tell me to begin the preparation for the upcoming high school admission examinations. Instead, each day I was told my daily and weekly job assignment. Most of the nights I slept in the farm so as to be able to have an early start on my daily work. While lying there in the haystack or out in the fields in the midst of the deadly darkness of the night I kept wondering as to whether I would be permitted to take the exams and if I were allowed to do so, would I be successful without any preparation?

Finally three days before the day of the interview early one morning I was unexpectedly awakened from my deep sleep by my brother John. Greatly surprised since that day I was supposed to be alone in the farm I asked him why he had come. With a gratified smile on his face, he told me that a message was received from the nearest town, Kastoria that the high school entrance examinations would take place in three days and that the family had decided that I should go and try my luck. He then shook my hand, wished me good luck, gave me a few words of encouragement and bid me farewell.

IV. HIGH SCHOOL YEARS

It was early in the morning when I began walking towards the village. All the villagers were walking away from it toward their work places and I alone was going in the opposite direction. I wondered then that if that was an indication that from now on I would be diverting from the path of my villagers.

Upon my arrival, my mother greeted me with her usual kind smile obviously happy that my dream finally had begun to be fulfilled.

After a delicious warm lunch I collected some of my old school notes and books and began to leaf through them. Page after page the material appeared familiar and yet blurred and distant since it had been quite some time since I had studied it. At sunset, somewhat despaired because my memory of the subjects appeared vague, I put everything aside and walked alone up in the mountains as I used to during my school years, wondering what the next three days would hold. The last night in my village before my venture, passed with the same thoughts. In the morning, my mother gave me the bag that she had prepared with food, bread, cheese, hard-boiled eggs, and pita pie enough to last me for three days. She kissed me, gave me advice and encouragement, and accompanied me to the main street to join the adult villagers who that day were going to the city. Once they realized that this 12-year-old boy was following them rather than walking towards his farm, they obviously started to wonder why he was going to the city. Did he know where to go? What was he going to do there? Of course I knew why I was going and what I

THE VOYAGE OF A SHEPHERD BOY

would be doing there, but since I had never previously ventured outside of the village or our farm, I did not know how I would do it. I did not know for certain where I would be staying while in the city, where the high school was, where the examinations would be given and what material they would cover, and above all, if I would be successful.

All these questions constantly occupied my mind during the four-hour walk from the village to the city, rendering everything around me a blur.

Once I reached the last hill before entering the city I could see, spread out into the distance, the big city of Kastoria, the Kosmopolis that I had dreamed of. A big lake with crisp clear water surrounded by big gray green mountains it engulfed a gray peninsula which was connected with the main land by a narrow neck of land about five hundred meters wide. The multicolor houses and other buildings were displayed on the peninsula, built with almost the same material and fashion as the houses in our village. On the crest of the peninsula at approximately the center of the city there was situated the clock tower dominating it. A philanthropist from our village donated it and it rang on the half hour and on the hour. Its sounds could be heard everywhere keeping all the citizens informed as to the time of the day. Along the bank of the lake there was a road lined by platani and other plants. Since it was a sunny day, the city with its surrounding trees was reflected in the lake, cresting a beautiful mirror image of an enchanting city.

The view of the city was overwhelming. Its beauty and size thrilled me and gave me great satisfaction knowing the opportunity ahead. Still, uncertainty and fear filled my mind. Where I was going to settle down and how I was to perform in the next two days?

Once I reached the city, I started my search for two boys from our village that had been in the city for the past three months to be tutored for the high school examinations. After some searching and wandering around the city, I finally located them.

They were surprised because they were not aware that I too would be taking the examinations and without any preparation. They felt sorry for me because I had not arranged any predetermined shelter and for my overall awkward situation, so they offered me to let me stay with them for the next two days. This generous offer was indeed manna from heaven for me. I now had shelter, I had food that I had brought with me and I had one day to find out where and at what time the exams were to be given, and how and on what my fellow students had been tutored. After a restless night, the next day I oriented myself as to what was to come up, and I spent my time wandering around the city like a zombie, admiring the surroundings and worrying about the exams.

The following day, in a stunned state, I walked the multiple stone stairs of the high school and soon I was led into a big room with one table and three chairs. The two examiners, Mr. Piheon and Mr. Liakos sat on one side of the table while I sat on the other. The examinations were on various subjects and material taught during the last two years of primary school. Everything, including the examiners faces was cloudy and blurred that morning but once the first question was fired the thick cloud which was sitting over my head was suddenly lifted and everything brightened. I was surprised that out of my confused and cloudy mind, the answers were emerging, thanks to my teacher Hatzizisis who as I have mentioned earlier had taught us not only the material required for primary school but far more. At the end of the examination period the examiners asked me for the name of my teacher and with a paternal pat on my back, they dismissed me. Next I was examined in composition and mathematics.

Initially I was elated due to the apparent success of the examinations and I was confident that I had passed. But as the time went on I started questioning my optimism. Before I left for my village I visited my aunt Katerina who was residing in Kastoria. She was a beautiful, loving, caring, and hard-working woman. She not only did all the housework but also worked in

THE VOYAGE OF A SHEPHERD BOY

the fields. She married a fine man, Theodoro Papargyriou, who then had come to teach in our village. Subsequently he became principal of a middle school in Kastoria. He was a quiet, serious, disciplinarian and wise man. In addition he was an advocate for my continued education. Two of their sons Petro and Dimitri were in schools in Athens. Petro was in a military school, Scholi Evelpidon and Dimitri was in the armed forces medical school. Subsequently both distinguished in the armed services. Petro retired with the rank of Two Star General and Dimitri became a neurosurgeon and he too retired with the rank of Two Star General. Argyri the third son was a junior in high school and their daughter, Fouli, was about four or five years old.

My aunt offered me something to eat and went on to tell me how happy she was to see me and how proud she was for the successful outcome of my examinations. I was pleasantly shocked with this news. How did she know the outcome of my examination so soon since its results were to be announced in a week? When somewhat restrained, I asked how she knew, she replied that the previous night while my uncle was playing cards in the café, his partner, Mr. Piheon, who happened to be one of my examiners, asked him whether he knew a teacher by the name Lazaros Hatzizisis in the village Dendrohori. He then went on to tell him that he had taught his students material beyond his wildest expectations. My uncle indicated that he indeed knew that teacher well and then casually asked who the examinee was. He was delighted to find out it was me. With this confirmation that I had done well, I returned to my village full of hidden pride.

The day after my arrival I was back to my previous work schedule but with a new outlook for my future. Since I now knew that this form of life was to continue only till the last days of September, every day, even the harshest and the most exhausting one was pleasant.

Finally, on September the thirtieth, 1938 at four o'clock in the morning walking with my father and with the mule loaded with firewood and food we began the journey to Kastoria. It was dark and very serene. The only noises that one could hear were the mule's footsteps and ours and, occasionally at a distance, the barking of the sheep dogs. Despite the darkness, it seemed to me that I could see far more than I could ever see before. Happy because at last I was going to high school, and fearful of the tasks that lay before me. I followed my father in silence searching in the deep darkness for answers to a myriad of unanswerable questions. After four hours of walking, we finally arrived at my aunt Katerina's house where I would be staying during the academic year. After a gracious welcome from my aunt and some discussion between her and my father, he left with no words of guidance or encouragement and revealed no signs of emotion upon leaving his son, save a stern well wish. Both of us tried to hide the emotions of the separation, but behind the stern mask of his face I could see his emotions, as I am sure he saw mine.

Although I was welcomed at my aunt's house, I was not at all acquainted with the family and therefore I felt alone, awkward and anxious about my new life in the city and the beginning of my high school studies. Argyri tried to assure me that I would do well and that I had nothing to fear.

At seven and an half o'clock the next morning, concealing my anxiety, we walked together to the high school. We climbed the long stone stairs, which led us to the flat schoolyard with a small church in the center, which was built in 1000 AD. The yard was full of new faces. Those who were returning to school were confident, joyful and socialized with each other. For the others like me for whom everything was new and unknown, the entire atmosphere was intimidating. Finally, the bell rang signaling that it was time to enter the building and begin introductions and classes. All the students, who were all males, lined up, each grade in three rows, and we went into our respective classrooms. The classrooms, apart from their size, were arranged the same way as those in our village and the students were seated in a similar manner with the shorter ones on the front rows.

Once we were seated, I somehow began feeling comfortable and confident. After all, I kept telling myself this would be nothing new only a continuation of my old school years. Therefore, by applying my prior work ethic, my school life would be as enjoyable and rewarding as it had been in the past. Indeed, this is what gradually happened during my first high school year.

The schedule was as follows; Monday through Friday we had classes from 8 am until noon, recess from noon until 1pm, and classes again from 1 pm until 5 pm. On Saturday classes were from 8 am until 12 noon. The remainder of Saturday and Sunday was reserved for rest. After classes, life consisted of homework for a couple of hours, playing various outside games with each other, walking around the city or the lake or down the main street along with many young and older citizens who were promenading. After dinner I would do more homework if I had not previously finished it, or I would read for pleasure. At my aunt's house everyone spent their free time reading. How much more conducive to learning could an environment be!

My time for real unwinding usually consisted of one weekend every month when I would escape to our farm or village. On Saturday afternoon, after dismissal from school, in order to release all of my restrained energy, I would walk for two or four hours either to our farm or to the village. It was indeed a very special time for me. Everything outside the city was beautiful and enjoyable. During winter the snowflakes overloaded the trees and the ground was covered with pristine white snow. During spring, the warm breeze, the sparkling blue sky, the fresh green trees, and the ever-present wild flowers filled the air with unlimited possibilities. During autumn the mist and the multicolored leaves gave me a sense of the changes that were to come. In addition, during my stay in the village I enjoyed the special meals that my mother always prepared for me.

So in my first year of high school, contrary to my fears, I slowly adjusted to my new environment and even managed to gain the class standing that I always enjoyed at my primary school. This course of action continued during my second year, which resulted in my designation as flag carrier for the class during the 25th of March parade commemorating the Liberation of Greece from the 400 years of Turkish occupation. This recognition was a great honor and one of the higher points of that academic year.

In the end of June the academic year ended successfully and I then walked two hours to our farm where every member of our family had begun harvesting the winter crop. I arrived at mid afternoon. The sky was crystal clear and the sun was blistering hot. Everyone was red-faced because of the extreme heat and lined up in a half bent position with a scythe in their right hand, tirelessly reaping the golden wheat.

After a short warm welcome, I was given the extra sickle that was available and I joined the harvesting line. While all of us were rhythmically bending up and down endlessly cutting the stems of the wheat, everyone wanted to hear about my experiences during the past year. After all, I was like a favorite son being sent off to prove myself and earn the pride of the whole village. I tried to answer their questions while I was hiding the discomfort from the heat and the manual effort to keep up with the harvesting pace. By sunset the skin of my face, arms, and legs was as red as a lobster, and yet somehow I enjoyed being back in the fields sharing the workload of my family members.

That summer passed quickly working constantly in the fields or taking care of the livestock. All my time was spent outdoors, even sleeping in the wheat fields, cornfields, meadows or mountains. The days were exhausting. From dawn until dusk we were expected to endure constant manual labor except for a few short breaks under an oak or walnut tree. The arrival of the night however, was like an arrival in an oasis. The almost unbearable heat dissipated, the sizzling noise of the crickets stopped and pale darkness lay over the land covered by a canopy of blue sky filled with a myriad of bright stars. Everything seemed as if it were standing still. The barking of some dogs or the voice of an owl only occasionally interrupted the surrounding tranquility. The warm ground covered with either the stems of the harvested wheat or with the green or dry grasses and a plain quilt was the most comfortable bed. No sooner had I lay down, covered with a quilt or a cape I was taken into a sweet, deep, uninterrupted sleep.

By October 1st I was back in the city of Kastoria beginning my third high school year. This time around a student from our village and I rented a basement room from a lively and most hospitable lady. It was the only room in the basement with a window at the level of the ground. The rest of the area was unfinished with a clay floor and fireplace, which we occasionally used to cook small meals, like scrambled eggs. The room had just enough space for two single beds, a small desk and a woodstove for heating but no means for cooling. We did our written homework on the one available desk one after the other and our reading was done either on the bed or outside in the yard.

Life in school had become comfortable and pleasant. I had the same schoolmates, the same routine as the previous year with of course new course material that was quite manageable and interesting. Unfortunately, this form of life lasted only for about a month.

1. SECOND WORLD WAR

On October 28, 1940 as I was walking early in the morning to school I noticed that something was different and uneasy in the street. There were no people rushing to work, no shouting from street venders for rolls or warm salep. Instead many soldiers with stern faces were rushing to various destinations. Upon arriving at the school gate I heard no student voices emanating from the schoolyard. While we were waiting to enter our classroom, most of us had the feeling that something was not right but we had no idea what was really going on.

With the arrival of our classical Greek teacher in our classroom it became obvious that something of great importance had occurred. His face was strained and his familiar early morning smile was absent. He told us that the previous night, the Italians had declared war against our country and had attacked us.

However, he consoling told us that we should not be overly concerned because we would prevail as we had done during our long previous history. Therefore he told us that our classes were suspended indefinitely and that it would be prudent for us to go to our respective homes until further notice, which hopefully would not be too long in the future. All of us were stunned from the shock and remained deadly silent until our teacher turned to walk out of our classroom. I then immediately returned to my rented room, picked up only my books and started walking westward from the city towards our village and the Albanian border. I had no sense of the gravity of this attack or a sense of the perilous events that would follow.

My walk home was not the pleasant one that I had so often during the previous two years. The uncertainty of the outcome of the war and the interruption of my school weighted heavily on me. I did not know when classes would resume or if I would be allowed to return to school. This unpleasantness was jolted deeper into my soul when half way from my village I first heard the sound of the heavy artillery from the Albanian border. The jolts became more piercing during my first night at home when I realized we were so close to the front line only about 20 kilometers away and, I could not only hear the sounds of the guns, but also I could see their firing flashes.

As to be expected, everybody's life was turned upside down. All the young men including my older brother Naum were drafted and they were fighting on the front line. The rest of us, although somewhat frightened continued our daily work, determined that we would prevail, despite the daily bombardment of our village during the first three days of the war. Our fear started to mitigate when we realized that the bombardment, for the most part, had been ineffective, resulting in only one death, two wounded, and minimal damage to our village. We became even more courageous when the sounds of the guns became weaker and especially when on the third day of the war, we saw prisoners hundreds of unarmed Italian soldiers marching toward our village. They were closely guarded and were being led by

THE VOYAGE OF A SHEPHERD BOY

a few of our soldiers to prison camps located in the interior of our country.

Finally, a few days later the sounds of the battleground guns could no longer be heard and the air raids stopped. Soon it became clear that not only had the attack of the enemy been halted, but also that now our forces were on the offensive pushing the enemy relentlessly back into the Albanian interior.

Everybody in the village resumed their routine work with greater efforts since all the most able men were at the front. In addition during the evening all the women would knit woolen sweaters, hats, gloves, and socks for our soldiers. Also, the men were occasionally called upon to use their own mules or horses to transport supplies from a neighboring village, which served as a provision center, for our army at the front lines.

Whenever our family was called upon to serve, usually my older brother John or my father volunteered because they felt that traveling in cold, rainy, or snowy weather was hard and risky for me. I, however, being eager to experience the drama that was unfolding in our mountains and being anxious to contribute to our nation's efforts insisted that I go each time our turn came. Finally, in the month of November when neither my brother nor my father could go, I was given the opportunity to experience what it would be like. It was a cold moist day with low dark clouds covering the entire horizon. I took our mule and in the company of several men older than I rode for an hour and a half to the provision center. We immediately loaded our mules with various provisions and started walking westward toward the front line led by one of our soldiers. By early afternoon the cold moisture turned to heavy cold rain. With a heavy woolen cape on my shoulders I followed the men not knowing where I was or where I was going. The road was rocky, full of water puddles making everybody's efforts exhausting. Finally, at dusk we arrived at a soldier's camp, which had small tents just large enough for two men to lay or sit in. It was located on the slope of a mountain with a freshly—smooth red clay surface. While the rain still continued we were told to unload our provisions.

Then we were given half a loaf of bread, a piece of cheese, one blanket a small tent for each pair of us and a bucket of oats for the animals. We were told to pitch the tents and make ourselves comfortable. Cold, wet, down to our bones, our feet soaked in the mud, we helplessly tried to put up our tent. Neither my companion nor I had done it before. A few soldiers saw our struggle and came to our rescue and in no time had pitched it and even made a small ditch around to prevent the water from entering.

We finally settled in our tent with one blanket on the ground and the other on our shoulders. Now protected from the pouring rain, we devoured our bread and cheese since we had not eaten since morning and tried to warm up and dry our clothes with our own body heat. After a while, our efforts proved hopeless since the water started coming into the tent, despite the protective ditch and the tent started leaking whenever we touched it inside.

My efforts to fall asleep were unproductive until the early morning hours when somehow I felt warmer, and with no water running beneath me or on top of me I finally fell asleep. At dawn, when I stepped out of the tent I realized why I earlier had felt drier. In the early morning hours instead of raining, it began to snow depositing a few centimeters, fresh snow on the ground and on our tent. Shortly after we awakened we were given some crackers and tea and we were told that we were no longer needed. This adventure taught me that the interruption of my school year that I considered a misfortune paled in comparison to the sacrifices and hardships that our men on the front were subjected to each day.

I returned home, and embarked on the daily tasks at our farm with the same determination and optimism that I saw in the courageous weather-burned faces of our soldiers. Autumn passed as well as the first part of winter and work continued as usual.

After the battlefield moved away from Greece into the interior of Albania, the life in our village returned to a relatively normal pace except for the daily worries for the well being of our soldiers. By January, all schools including my high school, resumed classes, and after a month or so of delay, I was allowed to return to the city of Kastoria and join my classmates. Even though, I was initially apprehensive and uneasy since I had missed classes for over a month it did not take me too long to catch up and adjust to the same level of comfort as in my previous school year. Unfortunately, this comfort was short lived. In early spring, rumors started that the German army would be coming to aid the failing Italian army and to offer retaliation for the humiliation that they suffered from the far fewer numbered Greeks. In April it was reported that the Germans had invaded Yugoslavia and were expected to rapidly reach our Greek border.

That weekend, feeling discouraged and somewhat depressed, I decided to visit our farm. It was a crispy comfortable April day with a clear blue sky and a bright sun. Yet to me it appeared dark, gloomy, and full of uncertainty and impending doom. After walking for two and a half hours I was greeted by our livestock, which was just arriving from their grazing in the mountain. The adult sheep and goats shaking away the burden of the heavy winter and the youngsters were free of care, full of joy, gobbling up their mother's plentiful milk, and sampling the fresh wild flowers and green grass. I began to wonder then if I was going to continue seeing them or if they were soon going to become sustenance for the Arian German invaders.

The next morning, while the livestock, full of energy and joy, were bursting out of the stockyard eager to start grazing the lush green mountain, on the other side of the river, periodically small units of our soldiers were marching away from the battlefield. No longer full of confidence and pride, they walked exhausted with mortally wounded souls. Their clothes were dirty and torn and their faces were strained, dark, unshaven and angry.

The following morning the Germans thunderously rolled down the same highway. As we feared, they reached our Greek Yugoslavian borders in less than three days. They appeared to move fearlessly and full of confidence thinking that the occupation of our country would take them less time than that of

Yugoslavia. Little did they know what lay ahead. Indeed, it took them over one month to overrun Greece and at a considerable price in casualties.

So the great victory of our armed forces against the Italians was sadly reversed by the German invasion, and Greek freedom and independence ended with the occupation by not one but three foreign forces, German, Italian, and Bulgarian. This three-pronged occupation subsequently resulted not only in physical destruction, but also, most importantly, in the social and psychological destruction of the matrix of everyone's life.

Each of the three forces of the axis took jurisdiction over different parts of our country. Our part, the western third of Macedonia, was delegated to the Italians, the eastern third to the Bulgarians, and the center third to the Germans, who, of course moved into the other parts whenever they wanted.

During at least part of the first year we in our village, due to its remote location rarely had to deal with the occupation forces. We encountered them when we visited Kastoria where the Italian garrison was stationed and when they were periodically making a short visit to our village in order to collect taxes on our products, wheat, corn, meat, and milk. Although these taxes significantly reduced our annual income, for the most part life was tolerable. The Italian soldiers were relatively friendly and not overbearing. Unfortunately this relative tranquility in our area was a temporary illusion and lasted only for several months.

2. UPRISING AGAINST THE OCCUPYING FORCES

During these months various forces were becoming entrenched. First, in the early part of 1942, sporadically there began to appear small units of armed men with multi-fashioned clothes, some in ill-fitting khaki and still others with civilian attire. They identified themselves as "andartes" or rebels taking their name from the gallant units, which had begun the struggle for the independence of our part of Greece from the Turkish occupation in the early part of the 20th century. They belonged to the EAM (Elliniko Apeleftheritiko Metopo) Greek liberation front, which was formed by the Greek communist party in September 1941.2 It was a secret political underground organization. These armed units of men were the secret fighting forces of EAM, which were called ELAS (Ellinikos Laikos Apeleftherotikos Stratos).

They initially claimed that their mission was to fight the occupying German, Italian, and Bulgarian forces and to liberate our country from their brutal tyranny. Shortly afterwards, it appeared in their slogan that, in addition, they were aiming to prevent the establishment of a monarch-led fascist government which really meant that they wanted the establishment of a true communist government after the occupying forces were expelled from our country.

From the beginning it was evident, at least in our village that their main aim was to position themselves in such a way that whenever the occupying forces left they would establish a communist regime in Greece. This appeared obvious because the individuals who formed the organizations in our village were known members of the communist party or communist sympathizers. In addition, in their talks and songs they exalted not only the communist leaders of Greece but also, of Bulgaria and Russia, never mentioning or remembering the previous heroes who fought for the liberty of Greece nor even those from whom they took their name "Antartes".

Shortly after the EAM established the nuclei of its organization, they also began to vigorously recruit those whom they considered receptive to their ideology. As they gained strength and control of the northern territory of Greece they began to manipulate everyone both physically and emotionally to get involved. The pressure upon the public to join their ranks eventually became harsh to the point that they openly began to state that whoever was not a member of their organization was their enemy. Eventually almost all of our villagers became members, the adults of the EAM a few of them of the organization ELAS and the teenagers of EPON.

At the same time when these organizations emerged, a few inhabitants of villages close to the Bulgarian and Yugoslavian borders, including a few from our village who were Bulgarian agents or sympathizers began to openly flirt with the occupying forces. Soon under the auspices of the Italians in our part of the country and the Germans and Bulgarians in other parts, they formed the Komitato, a Bulgarian-Slavic organization and many of them armed themselves forming the units called Komitatzides who fought by the side of the Italians, Germans, and Bulgarians. Although, they claimed they were to fight the strongly emerging ELAS, they began to terrorize everybody in the countryside and even killing those that they considered collaborators of any opposing them forces.

Amidst the early budding of the secret EAM organization in our village, a few Bulgarian sympathizers also joined the Komitato and began to forcefully push to organize the rest of the villagers with the Italians backing them. The unscrupulous force, intimidation and audacity reached such a point that one day they ordered that one adult male of each family should appear the next day in a neighboring village to be drafted. The majority of the villagers were disgusted and terrified at this prospect. In order to psuedo comply with their order and avoid any reprisal the eldest male who could not be drafted went to the designated meeting place. My father, instead of my brothers, who was then in his sixties also went. When the leaders of the Komitazides and their protectors, the Italians, saw only the elderly people appeared they realized that these villagers were unwilling to participate in their movement and that in fact their presence was a form of defiance against their order. Furiously they dismissed these seniors and all of them returned home.

The offence of the ELAS forces came in the form of an ambush against the Komitazides. The fighting became fierce especially at night. The villages where the Komitazides were stationed were frequently attacked by the ELAS forces that killed and abducted as many Komitazides as they could. In reprisal during daytime the Komitazides unleashed their anger and hatred against those that they considered supporters or sympathizers of the ELAS and against the "Garkomans," fanatic Greeks, looting their houses, confiscating their livestock, imprisoning and torturing the villagers. In essence life in the countryside became pandemonium. Everywhere there was fear, mistrust, and destruction.

Our village perhaps because of its remote location was spared of the looting and destruction but not of the suffering of the people. The Komitazides in one of their visits to our village took with them a few people as prisoners, tragically, including my brother Naum and my mother's best friend. They brought them to Kastoria and imprisoned them in the basement of their temporary prison quarters. Their quarters were stationed in one of the most beautiful buildings in Kastoria, which prior to the occupation of Greece was the home of one of the prominent families in the city. It was a three-story building with balconies for the majority of its rooms and a panoramic view of the city and its lake.

At that time I was attending classes in my high school in Kastoria. I was terrified when I heard that my brother was imprisoned. It was well known that people who were taken prisoners by the Komitatzides or by any of the occupying forces, German, Italian, and Bulgarian were submitted to merciless interrogations and severe corporal punishment. I wanted badly to visit and see him at least from a distance to see how he was yet the thought of encountering the traitors who were holding him was terrifying to me. I feared not only in what condition I might find my brother but also what might happen to me. I feared for myself because I was labeled by some as (Garkoman) a fanatic Greek, perhaps because I was still attending my Greek high school whereas eight of the ten boys from our village that we were in high school prior to the occupation had already left and a couple of them had joined the Komitazides. With that label I was very reluctant to visit my imprisoned brother.

Finally, after two days of deliberation with my heart pounding and my legs dragging, I walked up the rounding steep road, which led to my brother's prison. I thought it took me forever to reach it, although in real time it was only 5-10 minutes. The housing structure now appeared to me menacing, and not beautiful and bright as it looked when it was in the hands of the real owners. I thought I could hear inside the moaning and groaning of my brother and of the other prisoners. When I finally arrived at the entrance I was stopped by the guard and I was asked my name and purpose. When I replied the sentry's facial expression and his voice suddenly changed. It became harsher and angrier. For a short period I was so frightened that my vision became blurred. I was relieved when I was told to wait until someone would bring him out. As I waited outside the gate wondering about his condition he appeared before me accompanied by a guard. Limping exhausted and depressed, he approached the gate. There he was on the inside of the closed gate with me on the outside under the observation of his guards. We stood silent for a moment staring at each other trying to read in our faces what we were hiding in our soul and heart. Naum then asked with a wispherering voice, "How is everybody at home and how was my school going"? In return, I asked how he was. With somewhat cloudy eyes he answered, "Ok", and then our visit was terminated. As we walked away from each other, we simultanesly turned around to look at each other one more time before Naum was to be locked up again in the interrogation chamber and I was to return to my studies. All the deep emotions that this quick encounter evoked in me made it very difficult for me at least for a while to concentrate or to even rest. A few days later my brother was turned over to the Italian authorities. After they saw that all the charges against him were groundless he was thankfully set free.

The guerilla style war between the Komitazides and ELAS intensified. With ELAS growing exponentially in manpower and control of the territory many of the Komitatzides began to question themselves as to whether they were on the right side of the equation. Seeing that the power was shifting in favor of the ELAS forces, many of those who had not committed atrocities started to desert and to join the EAM or ELAS ranks. Similarly, the few men from our village who had become Komitazides were now unable, even if they wanted, to return to their previous life without repercussions from ELAS. So they blended into the EAM or ELAS.

The erosion of the power of the Komitatzides through killing or abduction continued to the point that they became not only irrelevant to their guardians, the Italians, Germans, and Bulgarians, but also a burden, because of the atrocities that they committed against even the peace loving civilians. Eventually the Germans executed some of the Komitatzides leaders and the rest of the followers were sent home to face or even join their previous enemy, the EAM and the ELAS. This end of the Komitatzides validated the Greek proverb "oli agapane tin prodosia ala kanenas ton prodotin" which means, "Everybody loves the treason but nobody the traitor".

From the inception of the EAM and ELAS our village as well as most of the mountainous villages in our territory were under their control. The occupying forces venture to visit us on few occasions. Unfortunately, however, whenever they did the consequences were bad. One day the Italian troops arrived early in the morning before the people left for their work in the countryside. They encircled the village and summoned everyone in the square. Then they ordered everybody to surrender any ammunition that they possessed within the next 24 hours. They also kept about thirty young men from the ages of 18 to 40, including my brother John, imprisoned them in a house where they again asked them if they had any ammunition to surrender. Of course none of them admitted to such a thing. This request was then followed by intense interrogations and severe corporal punishment. This mental and physical punishment seemingly resulted not only in confessions from some of them but also in the incriminations of others. Along with this group my brother John was handled in a similar fashion. For four days he was kept in isolation and was constantly submitted to interrogation and torture and finally he was set free.

After an arduous weeklong visit in the village the Italian soldiers left taking with them, fifteen of the young men that they had imprisoned. Shortly afterwards all of them were court-martialed by the Italian authorities and all of them except one were found guilty of treason. One was pardoned, seven were sent to concentration camps and the remaining six were executed by a firing squad.

Eventually the dominance of EAM and ELAS spread all over the countryside. The Italian and German forces were mainly entrenched fortified in the major cities. The inborn spirit of the Greek people to fight for their freedom coupled with the EAM's seductive slogans of equality, new political and economic system, and a better future life were enough for the majority of the people to embrace them. For the remaining Greek people who were skeptical or reluctant to follow the EAM, ELAS because of the Communist dominance of their actions, every form of persuasion, intimidation and sometimes punishment was utilized.

In time, in addition to the establishment of a separate organization for each age bracket, they established their own civil services, after they dismantled the old ones. They designated a new president and secretary of the village and established their own police and courts. The only criteria used to fill these positions were that the appointee had to be a newly inducted or a seasoned communist. The slogans that they were preaching, for equality and meritorious award, were only for propaganda purpose.

Practically every night after the villagers returned from their work the church bell would ring, not as in the past to announce the celebration of an orthodox liturgy, but to announce that a rally or meeting would be taking place. Everybody, no matter how tired from the day's labor was expected to attend it. Some of the villagers were enthusiastic about meeting together. Others somewhat disgusted, would reluctantly attend, and still others would try to find justifiable excuses not to go at all.

These rallies were aiming to brainwash the public and rouse their spirit with revolutionary songs and lectures and with false idealistic premises and also, in turn, to maintain discipline in the organizations with threats and intimidation.

While the growth of the EAM and its branches was going on, a new mini organization was sprouting within it. Since the communist party preached the complete equality of minorities, a small group of Slavophones, some of whom were previous Komitatzides, pushed the EAM to successfully adopt and establish within their own political organization the SNOF (Slavomakedonsky Norodny Osloboditelen Front).2 Subsequently, its Slavomakedonian members formed special armed bands within the ELAS ranks. The purpose of this organization was to establish an independent country that would consist of the Greek territory known as Macedonia and the most southern parts of Yugoslavia and Bulgaria, which would be united, when the Nazis left. However the harmonious existence of these SNOF Units within the ELAS group did not last long. Perhaps the leadership of EAM and ELAS realized that the plan for this separation of Macedonia from Greece was not only unacceptable but also unthinkable, to their non-core communist members, which were apparently the majority.

One morning while our family shepherd and I were following our grazing livestock in the mountains, young men could be seen running from bush to bush. Although, such a movement in the mountains had not been uncommon since the establishment of the ELAS group, this time they appeared more agitated and even frightened. Initially, we thought that they were members of ELAS. Upon inquiring as to what was going on we were told that they were members of the SNOF and they had come in conflict with their previous comrades, the ELAS, who were now chasing them. Indeed, shortly afterwards larger ELAS units appeared who were in pursuit of the SNOF. This conflict resulted in the resolution of the SNOF Organization with the majority of its members escaping to Yugoslavia. There they regrouped and trained with their new supporters, the Yugoslavian Communists in order to return later for the second round of conflict.

During the three years of Nazi occupation everybody's life went from bad to worse. First the economic devastation was of unimaginable proportions. The taxation and confiscation of consumable property by the occupying forces, the contribution of consumable materials to the sustenance of the ELAS, the unrelenting destruction of properties by the fighting forces all this lead to the almost complete depletion of food. Some of the villagers without sizable and diverse property to cultivate or without livestock had insurmountable difficulty in procuring food.

Our family, although we sustained a significant cut in our yearly income because of our substantial estate and farm property, we held on to the essentials for survival not only for ourselves but also had enough to help our extended family and friends. Salt, sugar, and kerosene were the main essentials that we could not produce and make from our regular farm products and livestock. Having extra food products as exchange thankfully we could procure these essentials from the black market. Secondly, the fighting and killing between all the competing forces, the Germans, Italians, Komitatzides and ELAS, although sporadic went unabated. The onslaught was not only between these forces but also between all of them and against the peace loving people. All this social and political division affected the relationships not only among strangers but also between friends and relatives. The love, support, and trust that existed before the war between each other dissipated. The original straight, carrying relation between people was almost gone.

To navigate in these treacherous waters of constant external and internal conflicts without giving even the slightest impression of disagreement with the thoughts and loyalties of other people and to avoid incrimination was next to impossible. The only way to accomplish this was to have a justifiable reason to stay away from the village and to avoid, as much as possible, any interaction with other people.

THE VOYAGE OF A SHEPHERD BOY

Fortunately, our family's life style was conducive to this kind of escape. Historically all male members of our family, day and night, raining, snowing or shining, almost always were living away from the village, working in the fields or attending our livestock in the mountains. I had an additional reason for staying away from any social interaction in the village. During the three years of the occupation of Greece I continued to attend my high school and to also work where my family needed me. In the summer and autumn I was spending my time in the countryside sleeping wherever I happened to be working. The rest of the time the duration of which varied I was in high school in Kastoria. This duration varied according to the will of the forces, which controlled our village at any given time and to a lesser degree because of my father's hesitance to let me go.

Despite the fact that I was almost all the time away from the village I could still not escape the persistent and intense pressure from members of the EAM and the communist party to include me in their revolutionary organizations. The first attempt was made in the very early period of their movement while the EAM, ELAS, and KKE (Koumounistiko Koma Ellados) were secretive underground organizations. One day while I was visiting my family from Kastoria for the weekend, late in the afternoon I walked to the village square and I met my grammar school classmates who were getting together as was customary to socialize. One of them, Dimitris Ziziadis (Dimitris Tarpofsky), who during the primary school years was one of my friends, took me aside. He was the son of a leading communist member, not only of our village but also of all Greece. In the darkness of the early night we began to walk back and forth in the churchyard and in a low secretive voice, he said that a new organization was emerging with the sole purpose of fighting for our liberation and for a government by the people, (Eleftheria, Laokratia, ke Isotita), meaning, "freedom, people's social republic, and equality."

All these beautiful words were enticing for everybody, but more so for a teenager. My pulse was racing and our footsteps hastened as if we were marching toward these goals. After a while we parted without mentioning what he expected of me. In the dark moonless night with the sky full of bright stars I walked home alone hearing only my footsteps and sensing my pounding heart. We did not meet again for quite awhile until I came for another family visit from Kastoria. At this encounter I could see that he was anxious to talk to me. As we walked alone again he immediately started the same subject. The more we talked the more it became apparent to me that he was trying to lure me into the communist movement. Although still the propaganda message of this emerging organization was appealing to me, I was wondering how they intended to meet its three objectives. I new that with intense and persistent fighting eventually we will be able to gain our freedom as so many times our predecessors have done in the past, but the feasibility of establishing a government by the people with equality for all was escaping me. Upon raising the question as to how this could be done, to my astonishment I was told that if all of us were organized and armed at the time of the departure of the occupying forces, we would be able to impose our will on all Greeks without and if needed with unlawful means, meaning fighting the people who would disagree. I was indeed shocked with this statement and my enthusiasm for what was emerging completely evaporated. That meant they planned to force the will of this organization upon friends, neighbors and fellow citizens. Then how was this promising organization differed from the Nazis? Of course I did not pose this question to him and after awhile we parted. Then my belief was affirmed that I should continue to stay away from any political organization, no matter how attractive it might appear and only to continue my pursuit of my high school education.

Although this posture was perhaps not patriotic I still felt justified because I could not be part of a movement, which was planning to impose its will upon the rest of the public.

After these two meetings with my friend, I tried to keep any contacts with him sparse, brief and cordial. He appeared to have accepted my wishes and said that he admired my dedication to high school education when everyone else, except for one other boy, had abandoned their studies. Over the subsequent two to three years we continued seeing each other sporadically but our previous closeness was gone. He clearly knew that I did not want to be involved in the EAM, ELAS, and EPON organizations and he certainly resented the fact that I did not join their political movement, but I liked to think that he secretly envied the directions of my life.

Over the next two years the pressure, direct or indirect for me to join the organizations of EAM continued. I was constantly urged to join them and sometimes threatened for my neutrality. I continued the course of life that I had chosen and I occasionally served them when I was ordered, including on one occasion, serving as a messenger from our village to another. Despite my token support the resentment towards me by many members of EAM continued to grow to the point that I was considered (Andidrastikos) reactionary, a label, which potentially could be accompanied with severe punishment.

During those years the power of EAM, and, as a result, its control of our village and almost all of Greece grew to unimaginable proportions. Simultaneously the mistrust and fear between most people grew and the EAM animosity towards those who had not taken their political side was unprecedented.

3. FIRST PRISON CAMP

Although I was considered reactionary and I had frequent, day and night indirect encounters with the ELAS forces I never feared for my life. This was because I believed that they knew that I was only guilty of wanting to stay out of politics and to continue at any cost my high school studies.

Unfortunately the resentment and even animosity towards me from the EAM and from some of our villagers continued to grow and clearly manifested itself in December 1944. That was when the Germans left Greece and the struggle for power and dominance between the various internal forces intensified. The ELAS forces controlled almost all of Greece and they wanted to impose their will and to establish their government, as they planned from the inception of their organization.

Instead the newly created post war government represented all the political parties. Because the EAM and especially the core communists were not happy with their share in the new Government they decided to take control of Greece by force. This resulted in the infamous fierce fighting in the capitol, Athens, between Greeks, it was ELAS versus our national and the British forces. At the same time the leaders of EAM, ELAS, and communist party in our territory decided to arrest the Greek citizens whom they considered enemies (prodotes) traitors. Since I was not involved in the EAM movement I knew that I was undesirable but I could never conceive that I was considered a traitor. Unfortunately, this was exactly what had happened. The communist commissars, supposedly acting on accusations against me from their party members whose identity I never found out, decided to include me in their round up of the supposed traitors. On a misty, chilly, December day, while I was preparing to leave home for our stockyard very early in the morning an armed member of the EAM police force stationed in our village knocked on our door. Immediately after I opened it he quickly slipped inside the house and stood beside me. This abrupt, invasive entrance surprised me but I dismissed it as another manifestation of their arrogance. He told me that I had to immediately accompanied him to the police station and that his chief wanted to see me. Although my surprise at his behavior was now accentuated, still I did not think that something serious was going on. Instead I thought I would be asked to serve them somehow that day. As we walked the cobble stone street leading to the police station I noticed that he always tried to walk behind me instead of beside or in front of me, since he was important authority. As soon as we entered the building I was led to an office. The two policemen who were there appeared somewhat agitated and the whole environment was suspicious. Something serious was going on but what? Still, being innocent of anything offending the EAM's political movement, I thought whatever was going on involved somebody else, not me. While we were standing there suddenly machine gun firing could be heard in the outskirts of the village and another officer subsequently burst in the room announcing, "The traitor tried to escape and we caught him." This event shook me up even more and I began to wonder. They shot and caught the traitor, then am I part of this? No, it was not possible, I thought because that prisoner was known for many years of his right wing leanings. Myself, I had no political affiliation and my only crime was that most of the time I was away from the village working in the fields or trying to attend my high school. This internal denial however evaporated when they brought in the "traitor" and two other men and they then locked me up with them in the confinement room. There in the dark room we all stood silently searching for an answer as to what was to follow. The three men were about twenty years older than I was, and appeared frightened but I was still thinking that nothing serious could and would come upon me.

Finally two policemen opened our door and told us that they would take us to a neighboring village where after we were asked some questions by one of their leaders, we would be allowed to return home. With an armed policeman on each side of the four of us, we were escorted along the main street of our village. As we walked along I was surprised to see several of our villagers on the side of the road staring at us. I walked with my head up without fear wondering what these people on this rainy, chilly day came out of their warm houses to see. Were they satisfied with what they were seeing? I did not hear any comments as we were passing by them and I did wish that they were not pleased. But then why were they out there enduring the miserable weather?

After an hour and a half of walking under constant, heavy rain, we arrived, soaked head to toe at the village where we were told that our misery would end. We immediately were taken to the local police station and locked in a detention room with several other unfamiliar males from our neighboring villages. Despite the crowd in the room no voice could be heard. Everyone had harsh and frightened face silently wondering what would follow.

After the long five to six hour ordeal of that day, I finally realized that being innocent of any wrong doing was no guarantee that all these escapades would be just an excursion to this village, as I was told. Indeed not too long after we arrived, in the midst of the heavy rain, we were herded out of the detention room and ordered to walk in line close to each other westward toward the mountain peaks, guarded closely by a new unfamiliar shift of armed policemen. The rain continued unrelentingly and as we moved toward higher elevation, and as the evening approached, the temperature dropped significantly. By nightfall we were given an old blanket and a piece of bread and we were locked in a house with broken windows, the location of which I never attempted to determine. All night the wind whistled as it was blowing through the broken windows. I tried hopelessly to fall asleep but the bitter cold and the uncertainty of tomorrow kept me awake all night. Overnight the rain changed to snow and by morning it had covered the ground. We were given some bread and tea for breakfast and ordered again to walk on as the previous day. As we continued to climb to a still higher elevation, the snow on the ground continued to accumulate and our legs were sinking in it up to our knees. Finally we arrived at the village Slimista that is located up in the mountains on the border between Greece and Albania. There we were imprisoned in a crowded school building with other men from our territory, and again we were given one blanket each to sleep on the wooden floor.

Our daily ration was a slice of bread a bowl of soup or a small piece of cheese, hardly enough to survive. Fortunately a man from our group had a distant relative or friend in the village that everyday brought him a loaf of bread. He shared it with the three of us, giving me, since I was a teenager, a larger piece. Most all the prisoners were adult males, except for me and three other students from our high school. We were constantly confined in the building and our entertainment was a transmission of communist and revolutionary slogans as well as threats toward

THE VOYAGE OF A SHEPHERD BOY

us and anybody who dared not to go along with their philosophy and actions. This happened at least once per day, usually at dusk, through a loudspeaker

The snow outside was deep, the temperature was freezing, and the days and nights were very long and emotionally suffocating. Although, the crowd was large and seemingly homogenous everybody was restrained and careful of what they were saying, careful not to comment on anything related to politics or our plot. There was an unspoken fear that there was a shadowy figure among us who was spying. My personal interaction was only with the three men from my village and the three high school students and even with them I was carefully restrained.

After couple weeks of detention, one day, late in the afternoon, several names were called on the loudspeaker including mine. We were directed to present ourselves to the office of the chief of the guard. Fearful not knowing what was to follow we entered his office. In a laconic manner and harsh tone we were, thankfully, told that we were free and that we could either leave immediately or since it was already dusk and snowing we could stay and leave in the morning. We were also told that upon our arrival at our homes we were to report to the central authority of the EAM.

Four young adults opted to leave immediately. They said that they were from neighboring villagers and they knew the territory well enough to walk home during the night. My heart was pounding; my legs felt light as feathers. I wanted to leave immediately also but I had no knowledge of that mountainous territory and my village was at least a day's walk from where we were. Upon asking the men who were ready to leave where they were going, the name of one of the villages, Inoi that was mentioned was not only familiar, but I vaguely remembered that one of our distant relatives was living there. I asked the man from that village whether he knew our relatives. He replied that he knew them well and that he would be glad to take me to their house. That was all that I needed to hear in order to venture out with them.

We left shortly after darkness fell. The snow was deep and there was no path to follow. We walked one behind the other alternating every so often the leader for relief. Our visual field was barely 20 feet radius and I had no idea where I was going. I followed my company with full trust even though I had not known them earlier. After a long arduous walk we parted, and the other three men walked southwards toward their villages and the fourth man and I continued eastward toward his village. After an additional hour's walk we reached our destination. It was well beyond midnight. Although I felt that I still had enough strength in me to walk home, hardly knowing my way and all alone, my better judgment was to spend the rest of the night there if possible and leave the next day. My companion then took me to my relative's house.

After repeated knocks on their door a middle-aged lady opened it. She immediately recognized my companion and asked him what she could do for us. He only had a chance to tell her my name. Although I did not remember having met her before she not only knew who I was but also what had happened to me. With extreme warmth and sympathy she immediately asked me to come in and insisted that under no circumstances would she permit me to continue my journey during the night. She thanked my companion profusely, as I did, for his great help and I told him I wished we could meet again later under better circumstances.

After she took me in, she threw wood in the fireplace to warm me up, brought me her family's clothes to change into, and fixed me a nice dinner. By then it was around 2 o'clock in the morning and she showed me my bed. The warm comfortable bed, the exhaustion from plowing all night in the deep snow to reach this destination and the guarded belief that I was free put me in the sweetest sleep that I have ever experienced. Late in the morning I woke up wondering whether all of this had really happened. My relative, with indescribable affection, gave me back my now washed and dried clothes and offered me a royal breakfast, fried eggs with small pieces of fresh pork meat and meat pie (Kreatopita). After I devoured as much as I could she gave me a package with food for the road and wished me Bon Voyage. This short wonderful visit with my distant relative was a breath of fresh air for me. Her indescribable gesture of hospitality lead me to believe that the majority of the people who were tangled in the web of the communist party and the EAM, as was her family kept hidden the old family and many others values; love, care and help for relatives and fellow citizens and even for those who were stamped as reactionaries as was myself.

After a three to four hours walk, I arrived in Kastoria and presented myself, as I was ordered to the command post of the EAM. The atmosphere at it appeared somewhat confused and in disarray. All the personnel of the post appeared subdued. When I told the guard what I was there for he shook his head and took me to his chief. Similarly, when I told the chief that I just came from Slimista and I was told to present myself to him, he too shook his head and with somewhat annoyed voice he said, "What they want me to do with you? You are free go to your home wherever that might be." By then it was close to sunset and I had four hours more to walk to reach my village.

Anxious to go home I left immediately wondering if I was really free? If yes what made that possible? What had brought about the subdued atmosphere at the EAM command post? The answers to these questions became apparent in the next few days when I found out that the ELAS was defeated in the battle of Athens and the attempt of the EAM and communist party to establish its own government had also been defeated.

I arrived home late at night. When my mother unexpectedly saw me she started crying from happiness. She knew, as all our villagers knew, that I was taken to a prison camp in Slimitsa. She also knew of some protests against my being exiled by a couple of influential members of EAM but she knew nothing about my release.

The next day I resumed the pattern of my life as it was before my capture. Members of my immediate family and a handful of villagers openly welcomed me. The majority of the other villagers I presume because of fear of being incriminated by the communist party and EAM, expressed their sorrow for my ordeal, only when no one else was present. The remaining few, including my grammar school classmate Dimitri, only cursory conversed with me when we faced each other. Their resentment and hostility towards me was clearly expressed in their face and bodily actions. I did not let this behavior bother me and I put aside all the previous events, neither showing nor expressing any discontent against anyone. I again began concentrating on my work and studies.

During most of the three and a half years of Nazi occupation our village was controlled by different and opposing forces than those, which controlled the city, Kastoria. Kastoria was always under the dominance of the axis forces, which included Italians and Germans, and also for a relative short period, their local collaborators, the Komitatzides. Our village was predominately controlled by the EAM, ELAS, except for intermittent short periods, when the axis forces elected to come and exert their authority. Due to these facts traveling to and from Kastoria was cumbersome, difficult, and sometimes impossible. As a result during my fourth and fifth grades of high school I was unable to begin attending on the designated dates. Every academic year I was delayed by two to three months. Fortunately, my teachers and the administration showed me extraordinary understanding and accommodation. Every year I was welcomed and inspired confidence that I would be able to cover the material that I had missed and be able to be promoted with my classmates.

After short periods of some difficulty I was able to catch up but I could attain excellent grades only in mathematics, physics and chemistry. This might have been due to the fact that I had a natural affinity towards these topics. I always found refuge in those subjects during the quiet times when I was with our livestock in the mountains or during many other leisure moments. Also, during the deadly quiet night hours in the farmhouse, I combated my loneliness and my occasional fears by reading in the light of the fireplace.

Although, this form of study may not appear to be conducive to learning, it helped me greatly each year to be able to catch up and surpass my classmates, at least in these subjects. During my senior year, due to even greater political turmoil, I was able to attend classes only about three months. Despite the lapse in attendance, I was to be permitted to graduate if I could successfully pass the examination on all the material that was taught during that academic year.

With intense studying during the last months of that academic year, I was able to graduate with high grades in the basic sciences and average grades in the other subjects. Although this achievement did not satisfy me completely it at least gave me hope that I could take the entrance examinations for medical school.

4. THE CIVIL WAR

After the defeat of the ELAS forces in Athens in December 1944 a peace treaty was signed with the provisions that everybody, except the National Armed Forces, would be disarmed, a government represented by all political parties would be established and a free election would follow. However, this political settlement again did not satisfy the communist party and the EAM. From the beginning they wanted to have a government of their own liking and not one representing the will of all the Greeks. They felt that the treaty was imposed upon them, which was indeed true.

With this argument, the ELAS chose to hide the majority of its weapons, instead of surrendering them as the terms of the treaty provided.

Also, many of its core members instead of returning to civil life went underground and continued to secretly work for their cause. As a consequence, although the life in the urban areas of Greece began to return to the Pre-World War II status, the rural mountainous areas such as our village was greatly influenced by the communist ideology and its underground followers (the Andartes) the Revolutionaries. This became evident in the first post-war national free elections in the spring of 1946. It was then that the communist party and the Andartes urged and even threatened our villagers to not participate in the elections. By doing so perhaps they were hoping that the results of the elections, which were expected not to be in favor of the communist party, would be interpreted as one-sided and the international community as illegitimate would discredit them. As a result, many of the villagers who still blindly followed whatever they were told by the communist party did not vote. Others like my brother John fearing the communist threats upon themselves and members of their families abstained from the elections. Such an action was unfortunately considered by some authorities of the National government as an indication that they were communist's sympathizers.

The rift between the communist and the other political parties over time grew deeper. At the same time the underground activities of the communist party and the Andartes intensified, becoming bolder and more confrontational. Utilizing the same means as they did during the Nazi occupation such as attractive slogans, (liberty, equality and government by the people) as well as revolutionary hymns, vigorous intimidations, threats and even punishment they increased the membership of the Andartes significantly. Slowly they began to openly challenge and undermine the legitimate authorities and the government rather than working together. Initially this lead to a war between the Andartes and the national police and later to a war between the Andartes and all Greek armed forces. This caused civil destruction equal to or even greater than that experienced during the occupation by the Axis forces. Respect for human values and even human life almost disappeared. During this terrible civil war everybody was suspicious of each other and was ready to incriminate the other for whatever was said, no matter how frivolous it was. The meaning of human rights did not exist in almost anybody's vocabulary. Everywhere terror and fear dominated and even execution was not uncommon.

THE VOYAGE OF A SHEPHERD BOY

These conditions unfortunately existed on both sides, the national government on the one side and the communist party and the Andartes on the other side. However, the national government side would eventually adjudicate and remedied every issue according to national law. The Andartes side, on the other hand they would adjudicate the issues according to the laws rules and values of the communist party and its local communist leaders. For example, two of our villagers who vanished during that period were arrested by members of the Andartes and communist party one night and were executed the next day without any fair trial, relying only on hearsay that they were traitors-prodotes. In addition it was said that their execution was carried out in a most inhumane manner. After extensive beating one man was stoned to death and the other was thrown in a deep crater.

At times the national police was zealous to arrest, and even torture anyone whom they suspected of being a collaborator or a sympathizer of the communist party or the Andartes. Nevertheless, eventually, the nationals in contrast to the Andartes, processed each issue through formal legal channels.

During the conflict not only was the whole social matrix of our country totally destroyed but also the tangible and real property of Greece. The Andartes took consumable material and houses were indiscriminately burned by each of the opposing forces.

Shortly after the establishment of the first post war national government my brother, John was drafted into the armed forces. My father then was in his late sixties and was unable to care for our property even with the help of the permanent and the occasional employees. Since the products of our property were the only available financial means to support me during my higher education we decided to postpone my education and sustain our property until John was released from the army. Then I assumed my brother's role. I had full responsibility for the care of the property as well as my parents. Although these responsibilities occupied almost all of my time I did not allow them to completely detach me from my books. As in previous years at every opportunity I always tried to review a page or a topic in my schoolbooks.

In the early years of my life I was dreaming of becoming a pilot or a physician. The first career as a pilot attracted me because flight would give me an uninhibited and seemingly weightless movement above and beyond every body else. This attraction was shattered during the war when I experienced the terror, fear and the destruction that pilots can cause. The second idea, the desire to become a physician came to me when my mother was inflicted with severe back pain, rendering her terribly uncomfortable no matter what position she assumed. At that time many relatives and friends gave her numerous remedies with no relief. There was no physician in our village. The closest one was in Kastoria, four hours away with the only available means of transportation being walking or riding a horse, mule or donkey.

Eventually, we put her on the back of our mule, and I led it and my father was following behind. After four hours of walking while constantly hearing my mother's moaning, we arrived in Kastoria. Along the way her pain and suffering was internalized in me. One of my mother's distant relatives, Dr. Sarandis Tsemanis, from a neighboring village was a physician practicing there. His office, with its distinct odors of various medications appeared to me impeccably ordered, and clean giving me the feeling of an oasis in our time of ordeal. After a warm greeting he examined my mother and gave her some medication. After a short period her suffering was measurably reduced. He gave us additional medications, instructed my father as to her subsequent care, and wished us a safe trip back.

The comfort of his office, the manner in which he treated us, especially my mother, and, above all, the relief of her suffering left me with an outstanding impression of this physician. While walking back home, and many times later, I thought that this would be the profession, which could provide the greatest and most precious service to the public, especially to people like our remote villagers. I thought surely this is the profession that I want for my self. This inner secret desire, although clearly unattainable then for me, guided and controlled all the subsequent steps of my life.

On the political front the growth of the Andartes forces continued unabated. This was accomplished mainly by vigorous and unscrupulous means of recruitment and the progressive return of the ELAS and SNOF forces from behind the Iron Curtain and especially Yugoslavia. Some of these men were those who went there during and after the first conflict. Simultaneously the villagers' support for the Andartes increased.

Some gave this support willingly and enthusiastically and others gave it because of fear of retaliation. This support made their movement easier. With the growth of the Andartes, their dominance spread. First it was limited to the mountainous countryside. Then it expanded to the mountainous villages, except for the village police stations, which were fortified. Slowly the power of the Andartes spread everywhere except for the major cities.

The National police station was located in the center of our village very close to neighboring homes and even attached to some of them. Initially, the policemen installed barbwire around it for protection and then they also built bankers. After several night skirmishes of increasing intensity with the Andartes the policemen realized that their location was not conducive to their adequate protection. They decided to relocate themselves in the new school building, which was positioned, alone on a dominant hill opposite from the village just in front of the vineyards. Before they made the move they fortified the school building. In order to do so they mandated that one able-bodied member of each family give two days of the week for the installation of the barbwire, the digging of the ditches and the building of the bunkers. Most of the work force was composed of young adults and teenagers who were supervised by policemen. For the most part, particularly for the single people, the work was fun, since we had the opportunity to work in groups with boys and girls of our age. One day while working, talking, and even flirting one very young single policeman made a comment with a sexual connotation. This embarrassed the girls and my cousin too. I was somewhat surprised by the remark and seeing the response of my cousin and the other girls I protested against it. Of course this insulted the ego of the young authority figure and so angrily he left to report me to his captain. At sunset he returned and ordered me to accompany him to the police station, an ominous sign.

Everybody in our group was expecting that I would be subjected to some form of punishment. When I faced the captain it became evident that the truth of the event had been distorted. Agitated, he asked me what happened in front of the accuser. I presented my version, which was unsuccessfully challenged by the accuser. The captain's facial expression abruptly changed. He justified my protest and went on to add that he would have done the same thing.

I wondered what the outcome would have been if this frivolous event had taken place, not with the policemen but with an Andarty.

While my brother John was gone my life was almost constantly away from the village, taking care of all the family farm and livestock chores. My social interactions were limited to our shepherd and to our other employees, my two cousins and a few of the villagers when they by necessity crossed my path going from one place to another.

In the mean time the organization and assertion of a new phase of communist movement continued. Fortunately this time either because I was always out of touch or because I was accepted as a steadfast in my views, I was not directly pressured to join this new communist uprising. However despite being out in the countryside day and night and as a result constantly being exposed to the Andartes, who were all over the countryside, I did not fear for my life. Also, although most of our villagers and even some relatives had distanced themselves from me and even

THE VOYAGE OF A SHEPHERD BOY

showed some animosity towards me, because again I was not part of this face of communist movement, I somehow believed that they would not cause me any direct harm. I felt that all the path of my life clearly indicated to them that I did not want any part of politics and that my only desire was to buy time until the opportunity came to go to the university.

Initially the recruitment of new Andartes was slow and voluntary but over time it became forceful indirectly and then directly. By spring 1947 our village police was confined only to its post that had become a fortress. The Andartes offenses against them became intensified. Everybody in the village was anxious, fearing something different was pending. Finally in June the Andartes began to forcefully draft many young males.

One day late in the afternoon after a hard day of work in the cornfields I returned with my cousin Kostas Symbas to our hay barns. Vangelis his older brother, happy to see us, anxiously told us that they (meaning the Andartes) have been looking for us everywhere. They want to take us by force. Fearing that they would come back we ran through the cornfields and disappeared in the dense bushes of a hill overlooking our farm area. We stayed there observing the territory until darkness fell. By then it started drizzling.

Having only a shirt on our shoulders we felt that we needed a blanket or a cap to spend the night in the bushes. We silently and carefully followed a path, which we knew it was unlikely for the Andartes to walk, we entered the house picked up a cap, and disappeared again in the forest. We selected a most inaccessible and densely wooded area on the same hill and slept there. That night in the frightening darkness with the rain falling over and running under me, I decided that the time had come for me to abandon the old plan, i.e. to continue to work until my brother John was released from the armed services, and leave permanently to find some way to take the upcoming entrance examination for medical school.

In the early morning while it was still dark and raining we both came down to the hay barns and I hid in the hay of our barn.

For a time I stayed in our hay barn, in its most remote corner covered with hay and pondered my future. After some time my father came to the barns from the village. By then the Andartes also had returned to look for me, and stood just outside of the barn where I was hiding. As soon as my father arrived they asked him where I was. He said that he did not know, but since our other mule was here grazing, my son must be somewhere in the mountainside with our livestock. From my hideout spot I could hear the conversation and wished that they would not accompany my father when he entered the barn. To my great relief they were convinced that I was not there and they left to look for me elsewhere.

When my father opened the barn's door alone I stuck my head out of the hay. Relieved that I was there, he said that the bastards, the Andartes, were looking for me. I told him that I knew it and I had been hiding from them since the previous evening. Then I said this struggle must end. This is as far as we could go this way. There could be no hope in running and hiding. We had to change plans and whatever happened, happened. I told him I must leave now for the village to assemble my books and notes and whatever else I needed and early the next day I would leave for Kastoria. My father knowing deep in his heart that this was the best and only choice for everybody and especially for me, with a somewhat choked voice, something that seldom happened to him, he said Yes this is what we must do but what will happen to you? How will you sustain yourself? Will our family be able to provide you any help? I did not answer his questions. Instead we emotionally embraced each other and then he stepped out of the barn to determine whether it was safe for me to exit. I briskly walked out and before too long I disappeared in the forest. After two hours of climbing and descending the mountain, which is interposed, between our village and the farm, through unusual safe paths, I reached our house.

My mother was greatly surprised to see me early during the day. I explained to her what had transpired and what was to follow. She was relieved, hearing that from now on I would be away from the turmoil, which existed in our village and all around. Neither she nor my father expressed any concern as to how they would manage the property or what their own repercussions might be from the Andartes as a result of my secret departure from the village. I assembled my books and notes on the subjects that I expected to be examined on at the university. My mother prepared food supplies to take with me and arranged for my sister Vasiliki to take our mule loaded with supplies on the conventional road to Kastoria while I was to take a different path (Figure 4).

Figure 4
Shortly before I left my village to take the entrance examination for medical School.

I was full of mixed emotions. I was very glad to be leaving an environment full of suspicion, mistrust, animosity and danger. I was sad because I was leaving my parents perhaps forever and with so much workload and so many other problems. I was also very apprehensive and even frightened because of the complete uncertainty that I was facing but still happy because of the remote possibility that I would be able to attempt to attend the university. I tried to sleep that night but all these emotions as well as the fear of being caught by the Andartes when I was walking alone in the darkness to go to Kastoria not only kept me awake, but constantly sweating and turning from side to side all night.

At three o'clock in the morning my mother came to my bedside and awakened me. She tried to project confidence that everything would go well but I could sense her anxiousness and fear. She had already prepared my breakfast but because of my agony I could not swallow anything. We embraced each other with a premonition that this would be the last embrace for a long time to come, as indeed it was.

In the deep darkness I dashed out of the house and in no time, through the fields, I reached the gorge, which begins a short distance from our house and ends down in the valley about two hours away from Kastoria. I could hardly see even a few steps in front of me. I walked and ran through the bushes going through the most unapproachable areas at the side of the gorge with a sense of security that there at night it was most unlikely that the Andartes would be trailing. Every bush looked as if it was a human shadow and every noise sounded like men's footsteps.

After more than two hours of agonized walking I reached the outlet of the gorge away from the common stepping grounds of the Andartes. The darkness of the night began to dissipate, and with it all of my fears of being intercepted by the Andartes dissipated. I waited for a while to meet my sister at the site where my path merged with the regular road that she and everybody else were following toward Kastoria.

When she arrived my sister was relieved to see that I made it but many of her companion villagers appeared suspicious and aggravated to see me there, even after my sister explained that I was going away to take the entrance examination for the university. Perhaps this reason was not justification enough for walking away from the "noble" struggle of the Communist Party! This attitude did not surprise me, but it did hurt me. Nevertheless, I was occupied with other concerns, like where was I going to stay in Kastoria and I ignored them.

Because of my abrupt departure from the village I had made no housing arrangements. The only accessible temporary shelter that I could think of was my aunt Katerina's house. When I arrived she welcomed me as always, and asked me how everyone was in the village. Once I described to her all the events she offered for me to stay with her family until I left for Thessaloniki for the university. The Papargyrious' took me in as a member of their immediate family. Indeed, by then I felt and I still feel that I was part of their family.

Shortly after I left the village all the young males were inducted into the Andartes forces. Some of them went willingly, euphoric from the constant indoctrination and from the rapid expansion of the power and the dominance of the Andartes, yet others like my cousin Kostas were forcefully taken. They were all thrown into the battlefields without substantial training and preparations and shortly afterwards many of them were killed including my cousin Kostas.

In the meantime the fighting, which had become a civil war, was escalating. Initially it was between the Andartes and all the police forces outside of the major cities and against small isolated units of the armed forces. By the summer of 1947 it had blossomed to an all out war between Andartes and all of the national forces, even those stationed in the cities.

The police force of our village had then been completely isolated from all national forces and, therefore, vulnerable and unable to carry on any of its duties and so it withdrew into the city. From that point on the visits of our villagers to Kastoria became very difficult and extremely rare. Then it became clear to my father that the possibility of their coming to Kastoria and providing me with some financial support soon will be impossible. Thus one night shortly after midnight he herded about 10 heads from our livestock and during the darkness brought them to Kastoria. I was surprised when I saw him in the market in the morning and asked him what he was doing. He said, this is my last opportunity to give you some money and this is the last time that we will see each other for a long time to come, if ever. He sold the livestock gave me most of the money and said, Take this, follow your plans as closely as you can and I am very sorry that from now on we wont be able to help you farther. We embraced each other and hastily he turned to go back to our stockyard. I walked slowly behind him along the northern shore of the lake following his shadow as it slowly faded in the distance. We did not see each other again until eleven years later.

I walked back to my room with the feeling of a sailor lost in a fierce sea, with only the knowledge of where he wanted to go and the unyielding will to do it but with no means and no idea how to accomplish his goal. I was very concerned because I had no guidance as to the dimension of the material that I needed to study for the examinations. I knew that soon I should be leaving for Thessaloniki but I had no idea where I was going to stay and how I would support myself. The money that my father had given me was a welcome relief but it would only be enough to take me to Thessaloniki and perhaps last for a short period afterwards. However, recalling that now at least I had the opportunity to try to fulfill my dreams and to move away from the chaotic situation, which dominated all the countryside, I felt that I was one of the most blessed young male in the world. With these tormenting thoughts and emotions I spent all my time studying, except for a couple of walks a day in the marketplace or by the lakeshore.

While I was proceeding with all the preparations, and examining and reexamining my overall situation, I began to seriously doubt that my dream of becoming a physician was attainable. First, because of my disorganized studies and unguided preparation for the examination, my chances for successfully competing for the most competitive entrance examination in the university was very low, if any. I was told that there were over five hundred applicants for sixty positions. Secondly, even if I were to be successful in the examinations, sustaining myself without support for the six years duration of medical school began to appear to me impossible. As a result I started thinking of an alternative.

My aunt's husband, as I mentioned earlier, was a primary school teacher. He appeared to be very satisfied and happy with his profession. The study period for his profession was two years in the teacher's academy, which was also located in

Thessaloniki. Therefore, I decided that I would try to take the entrance examinations for both the teacher academy and for the medical school. My thought process was based on the hope that I would secure my admission at least in one if not both schools and depending upon how the future would evolve I could then decide which path I would follow.

With these new initiatives about six weeks or so before the designated date of the examinations I decided to leave for Thessoloniki. This move could give me enough time to settle in the big city before the examinations. I also wanted to relieve my relatives from my imposition of staying with them, even though, as I stated earlier, they gladly took me in and treated me as a member of their immediate family.

V. FIRST STEP TOWARDS HIGHER EDUCATION

Because the fighting outside of Kastoria was raging travel from that city to Thessaloniki was limited to once every two weeks and even that was under major army escort. On the day of departure I boarded the bus, which was positioned in the center of the convoy. In front of the convoy traveled the mine detecting armored car followed by a truck loaded with a unit of armed forces, then came the Lorries, followed by the buses with the civilians, and lastly was another small unit of armed forces. The traveling was slow, eerie and even frightening. I thought then what a tragedy, we in our own country could move and travel in only a limited corridor, the main highway and under guard. Sadly, even that limited corridor was later challenged when we reached the peak of the mountain that we had to pass before we descended into the valley of Thessaloniki. There the slow movement of the convoy was brought to an abrupt stop in order to disarm the hidden road mines. Shortly afterwards machine guns began firing from all directions. All armed personnel spread around the convoy to protect it. After several minutes of firing, fortunately with no dead or wounded, the Andartes disappeared in the mountain brush. We continued our trip and by late afternoon we arrived in Thessaloniki. The armed forces went to their barracks and our bus stopped in the commercial district, at the bus station.

I picked up my bag and walked around to find a cheap hotel to spend the night. I settled in an inexpensive but noisy room. Shortly afterwards I left my room and began to walk endlessly trying to extinguish my agony and anxiety. After touring the center of the city I returned late at night to my room. It was quiet then even with open windows, since the market was closed. I tried to fall asleep but the anxiety about the pending examinations and about my physical sustenance kept me awake. In the midst of the search for a solution for my food and lodging I recalled my mother saying that her best friend Iordana Karatza had gone to Thessaloniki to find a way to immigrate to Australia and join her son. She was supposed to be living with one of her distant relatives who had settled there for many years. In addition of being my mother's closest friend, my mother had generously helped her during the occupation by the AXIS Forces. During that time my mother's friend did not have any livestock or significant cultivable property, therefore, was deprived of many food products. My mother knowing her situation at every opportunity, especially during holidays or weekends had given her food and food products as gifts. I had met Iordana during her frequent visits to our house and she appeared most appreciative of my mother's friendship and support.

These recollections gave me a glimpse of hope from a friend in the city, and so I finally fell asleep. I was awakened early in the morning by the bustling noise of the surrounding market. First I walked to the medical school to determine the exact place, date and time of the examinations and to make sure that my application papers were in order.

Then I took a long walk to the teacher's academy to see if the date for the application for the entrance examination had expired and whether its dates of the examinations did not conflict with the examinations for medical school. I was pleased to hear that the dates of the examination for the two schools were different and although the date for the application for the teacher's academy had expired I was allowed to apply due to my special circumstances. However, I was disturbed when I was told that with my application I had to submit the original high school diploma, which I did not have because I had submitted it with my application to the medical school. I was then faced with the dilemma of either abandoning my plans to take the examinations for the academy or making a false statement saying that I only had a copy of my diploma because the original was lost in the village during the war years. With a guilty conscious I chose to make a false statement rather than lose the opportunity to compete. With that shaky false argument I was permitted to participate in the upcoming examinations.

The next morning after I found the address of the relatives of my mother's friend and walked to their house to inquire about her. Fortunately, she was there visiting them as she did very often during her stay in Thessaloniki. As was expected she was surprised to see me and pleased to hear that I came to take the entrance examination for medical school.

After I answered a myriad of questions about everything and everybody in the village, she said I am sorry because I cannot offer you a solution to your many problems but I will try to secure housing for you. The next day she contacted a past grammar school teacher of our village who was a friend of hers and a friend of my brother Naum. He had a farm in the eastern outskirts of the city and he offered me his hospitality while my mother's friend, Iordana, tried to find, among her acquaintances, a suitable permanent shelter for me. Both the grammar school teacher and his wife were over sixty-five years and retired. I offered to help them with the farm work but they refused and stated that I should concentrate on my studies and all my other issues.

The next morning and each morning afterwards, after a breakfast of homemade cereal provided by my hosts, I walked to the streetcar station and I began hopping from car to car to avoid payment to the conductor until I reached the market place. There after some searching I frequently found a temporary job, usually moving produce and worked until noon. This work frequently secured me a lunch and a meager income. Then I went to either the library or to my room to study the rest of the day and part of the night.

After several days my mother's friend came to take me to my new shelter. The house where I moved was located in the eastern site of the city somewhere between the university and the Teacher's Academy. The hostesses were two nice middle-aged ladies, acquaintances of my mother's friend. They were unemployed and they appeared to have a meager income. They were living in a small apartment with two bedrooms, a small kitchen and a small area used as a den and a corridor connecting the two bedrooms with the kitchen. My room was a small area of the corridor partitioned by a moveable folding wall. It appeared that it was improvised to accommodate me. Both ladies were kind and generous. Although they were living a very frugal life they frequently offered me a plain breakfast, homemade crackers and mountain tea or an afternoon snack, usually a piece of bread and cheese.

I continued my daily routine of doing some work early in the morning and studying mostly in the library in the afternoon and evening. This arrangement gave me some hope that for a while at least I would be able to partially sustain myself. But the inconsistency of the availability of part time work in the market and especially the thought of the upcoming examinations kept me constantly awake at night.

The agony about these issues was always with me, wherever I went, whatever I did. The nights were especially difficult. Then in the dark quiet atmosphere, the thought that perhaps the next day I would not be able to procure even a meager income and the doubt as to whether I was indeed prepared for the examinations, made me sweat profusely. Then I had to spend considerable time to convincing myself that even with these adversities I was still very lucky to be where I was and finally I could fall asleep.

At last the date for the examinations for medical school arrived. After an even more agonizing night, I rode the streetcar to the university. Amidst the streetcar's clinking sounds I foolishly tried to recall some of the facts about the topics that I would be tested. My mind went completely blank. This event, of course increased my agony. The fear and uncertainty continued until I arrived and the topics that we had to describe were announced. Instantly then my confusion cleared as if all the clouds were lifted from my mind and I began to recall the necessary material. I finished the test on time and although I was not certain of how I did, overall I felt relatively good about my performance. We were examined for four consecutive days, one subject a day. Each day evolved in a similar manner. Encouraged by my performance, but totally uncertain about the outcome of the examinations, I subsequently took the testing for the teacher's academy with similar misgiving about them.

From then on I devoted everyday to my search for a job and began to fell somewhat more self-sufficient.

The results of the examinations for the teacher's academy came out soon after the testing and I was enrolled for the academic year, which would begin soon. This success gave me a big lift although I did not have the results of the testing for medical school, I had made my first substantial step forward.

1. MY ARMED FORCES SERVICE

In the mean time the war between the national forces and Andartes became more fierce and brutal resulting in numerous daily causalities. In addition to the constant fighting in the countryside there were frequent, major destructive attacks against major cities.

Up to that time all males of draft age who were enrolled in a school of higher education were exempted from service. However the ongoing great daily loss of young men on the battlefield resulted in a public outcry and protest against the exclusion from service of the "privileged and elite" group of young males in the schools of higher education. The government was thus forced to revoke the law and ordered all eligible students to be drafted.

Then I too became eligible to be drafted. Along with all the draftees I was notified to be at the Thessaloniki harbor from where a transport navy tanker would transfer us to the city of

THE VOYAGE OF A SHEPHERD BOY

Volos. I faced this event with mixed emotions. On the one hand I was distraught because now that I had the opportunity to continue my higher education I had to divert again and happy on the other hand because all the worries about how to survive in the big city and how to continue my education were over. From then on, at least for two or more years the armed forces would care for me and when the tenure of my service was over I would be better prepared to face my challenges.

I visited my previous host, the grammar school teacher and thanked him and his wife for their great help and support.

Also, I visited my mother's friend. She was very pleased to hear that I was accepted in the teacher's academy, yet also concerned for me since I was drafted and was going to war. I had no words to thank her, my gratitude was enormous. She had been like a life jacket, which helped me, swim in the difficult waters during the past two or more months. I did not see her again until thirty years later when I was in Australia at an international meeting. It was an emotional and gratifying meeting for both of us.

At times I recall a proverb that my mother quoted whenever we talked about her generosity toward her friend and many other people. "Rixe piso sou na to vris brosta sou," meaning throw something behind you in order to find it in front of you. In other words be generous and helpful to everybody and somehow in the future you will be rewarded. I was certainly rewarded for my mother's kindness and generosity.

Finally, I thanked my current gracious hostess; the two very kind ladies and I threw away all my books, notes and my very few other possessions and walked to the harbor. There the transport tanker was anchored.

The square at the harbor was packed with people and the atmosphere was very emotional. Mothers as well as other women and girls were embracing the draftees and crying, and the young men too were struggling to control their emotions. I somehow felt no sentiment, no reservation, and even had no concern about this new phase of my life.

Soon we were packed in the cargo area of the ship and the next morning, October 21, 1947, we arrived at the K.V.E. Volou, where we were assigned to our respective units and were given our uniforms, blankets, rifles, etc. For the first few days we were occupied with orientation and training. A few days later several of us unexpectedly were ordered to surrender our rifles and get ready for departure. Immediately rumors spread that those of us who were called were considered undesirables and that we would be taken to a concentration camp.

I became furious, I thought this couldn't be true. Three years ago the EAM and the communist party sent me to a prison camp and now our government authorities wanted to take me to yet another one. How could I be undesirable and even dangerous to both opposing forces? I immediately told my sergeant that before I surrender my rifle I wanted to speak to our captain. With great reluctance he took me to his office. After the usual formalities, in essence, I told him that I was obeying the order to surrender my rifle but before I did that I wanted to know why and where I would be taken. He avoided answering me. Then I pointedly asked him, whether I was considered unsuited and undesirable for the armed services or was I perceived as a communist or sympathizer to the Andartes. Also, I asked him whether he was aware that not only I was not a communist but that in 1944 during the Athens battle between the ELAS and the national forces I was taken to a concentration camp in Slimista by the EAM and the Communist Party because I was considered dangerous to them.

I finally suggested to him to delay my departure and send an urgent message to the police station of Kastoria and to ask them for my intelligence file, to determine why I was considered undesirable.

He replied that he would like to do all that but he could not. Which perhaps meant that it was not his job to do that.

Fuming with anger, I saluted and thanked him for giving me the opportunity to protest and with misty eyes, whispering, I said, too bad for both of us. It was certainly horrific for me

THE VOYAGE OF A SHEPHERD BOY

to be unfairly smeared and to have to endure the concentration camp of the Island Makronisos and it was bad also for the armed forces to take out of action a valuable soldier.

2. SECOND PRISON CAMP

After a few hours I was back again in the cargo area of another tanker only this time to be taken to the concentration camp in the island of Makronisos.

Still raging from anger I tried to reason as to why my captain did not do anything on my behalf. His mission, I reasoned was to train as best as he could and as soon as possible his new recruits to fight the Andartes. He therefore had no time to investigate whether or not the information that he received about me was true or not. Also he could not afford to keep among his men one who was stamped by the intelligence service as lacking trust since it was well known that soldiers in the midst of a battle were occasionally defecting to the Andartes. Perhaps I was rightly delegated to a special group of people who had the time, the means, and the expertise to do the screening. With this rationalization and believing that soon after I arrived at the island, I would be exonerated, my anger was somewhat resolved.

As the night progressed the conditions in the cargo area became deplorable. Numerous men were packed like sardines, many of whom became seasick and vomited all over the place. The emissions from such a crowd and from the vomitus and also the limited ventilation of the area made the atmosphere unbearable. By mid morning October 30, 1947, I was glad to get out even though I was going to a concentration camp.

Makronisos, meaning long island, is an uninhabited long island, mountainous, dry and barren with sandy red clay and a few dry bushes and with no consumable water. It is usually windy and hot during the summer and very chilly in late autumn, early spring and especially during winter. It is located immediately east of the Cape Sounion and of the lower eastern coast of the mainland of Greece. A boat ride from the island to Lavrion, a city at the tip of Cape Sounion takes less than an hour.

87

Hundreds of tents were lined next to each other in the mid section of the island, from the seaside, up the slope of the mountain. The tents were divided into three major groups. Each group was about fifty feet away from the other and each sheltered a company of soldiers. Just above each group at a short distance were several other tents. These were for the captains, their aids and the army police. At the top of the hill, above all the tents were the tents housing the major, his aids, the office of reformation, and the elite guard for all the battalion. The police army was composed of men who were brought there for exile and they were subsequently "rehabilitated". According to rumors all of them had active participation in the EAM, ELAS and communist party, and some had incriminating careers. Of course all of them had denounced all these alliances. They were not armed, instead they carried bats and many of these brutal men used them ruthlessly. The soldiers of the Elite Guard were fully armed and it was said that they too had been previously "rehabilitated."

After we disembarked we were divided into three groups. Each group was assigned to one of the three companies. I was assigned to the second company Skapaneon. On the day of our arrival after supper and before dismissal for the night, all the newly arrived soldiers were told to assemble in front of the captain's tent. At the entrance of the tent a policeman stood guard. Two other policemen lined us up one behind the other and the fourth one was taking one soldier at a time into the captain's tend. I was far back in the line. Each man stayed in the tent different lengths of time and when they exited all of them were unhappier and more frightened than before they entered. Despite this scene not only was I not majorably disturbed, but also I was even optimistic because I thought at last I would have the chance to speak to someone who will be willing to act on my behalf. Unfortunately when my turn came to go in I could not have been more disappointed and angered.

The captain, Mr. Liakakis, was a short statuted, harsh and stubborn man. After the formal salute he asked me if I knew why

I was sent there. I replied perhaps because I have been perceived as untrustworthy but I do not know why that is. His quick and harsh answer was that he knew why and that was because I was involved with the EAM and the communist party. With a stern voice, because by now my Greek blood was at a boiling point, I told him I was sorry because he was badly informed. How is it possible for me to have been involved with them, since they at the end of their first era, in 1944 at the time of the Athens battle between the ELAS and our national armed forces, took me to Slimista to their concentration camp? He did not acknowledge my answer but instead he asked me to sign a declaration of repentance and denouncement of my past. I told him that I could not do that because I was proud of my past and that I was not involved with the EAM or the communist party and I had not been nor am I a communist. Furious, he dismissed me.

Deeply distraught and disillusioned, I walked to my tent doubting whether my captain was there to objectively and impartially resolve my issue, as I previously expected. It appeared that his main aim was only to make me sign the declaration of repentance, and denunciation of my past. He had no desire to objectively find the real truth.

The next morning, while I was having my breakfast on the rocks of the coast I was greatly surprised, to see my brother John waving at me from a distance. After about two years of service elsewhere, he was brought to exile a few months before me although he too was not involved in the EAM, ELAS or communist party movement. The previous day he apparently had been watching our disembarkation from the tanker, and he was very surprised to see me there. Since that moment he had been trying to find the opportunity to talk to me (Figure 5).

Figure 5
**In the concentration camp in the island of Makronisos,
with my brother John.**

He was assigned to the first company and his tent was a few hundred yards from mine. I wanted to go to meet him, but a casual visit from one company to the other was not permitted. One way to have such a visit was by obtaining a permit from the company's police, a way that neither one of us wanted to take because of our fear of recrimination. Another way was to pretend to walk to a mutually used site such as that which was separating the two companies or at the canteen. Even in those circumstances the police was closely watching, and if the visit was prolonged, it was immediately interrupted by one of the policemen.

Our first meeting was on the mutually used ground by my brother's and my company, i.e. the space that separated our two companies. It was an emotional, very brief meeting, just enough

THE VOYAGE OF A SHEPHERD BOY

to inquire about each other's health and about any news from our parents. A few days later we met again at the same area but this time we were spotted by one of my company's policemen. Immediately he came to us and ordered me to return to my tent.

He followed my footsteps and instead of allowing me to go to my tent he took me to the "mandra" or barn. It was a small area surrounded by bare walls and it was mainly used as a torture chamber. With the indictment that I had violated the rule concerning visiting soldiers from another company, I was subjected to corporal punishment without it being reported to our captain.

Few days later, immediately after our dismissal for the night, a few of us were ordered to come to the captain's tend. There as on the first night of our arrival, one by one we were taken in. The tent was dimly lit and its atmosphere intimidating. There under the threatening eyes of the army police the captain made few statements of indoctrination and threats and asked me again to sign a declaration of repentance and denunciation of the past. I again refused and added that I would only be too glad to sign a declaration that I was never involved with the EAM and communist party, and I had never been nor am I now a communist. After considerably more heated debates on this issue he turned to his secretary and asked him to prepare a document stating that I was never a communist and that I was not involved with the EAM, ELAS, or EPON Organizations. Agitated then he asked me to sign it, which, perturbed, I did and he then asked the nearby policeman to let me go. I left hoping that this would satisfy the captain and that my ordeal would soon be over. Unfortunately, I was wrong. My nightly visit to the captain's tent was repeated until at last he was transferred elsewhere.

A pleasant appearing young man, Mr. Theodorou replaced him. I thought then my situation would change for the better. Tragically I was wrong again.Sometime after his arrival again at night I was called to the captain's tent. We went over the same questions, intimidations and demands as in all previous visits, and at the end I made an emotional plea, I asked him to make a request to the police of Kastoria to provide him with clear documentation as to how I was involved with the EAM and or the communist party. Then if indeed I was guilty he could impose upon me any form of punishment that he pleased. With cloudy eyes, I left without being touched by the policeman on guard.

About a month or so later I was called again by the captain who asked where I stood. I told him I stand where I have always stood, and I would like to ask whether you had made any inquiry and what was the outcome. Without answering me I was dismissed. I did not know if he had made the inquiry, and if not why.

A couple of months later he was transferred to the front line. In one of the battles with the Andartes in our village mountain Malimadi, he was wounded and hospitalized in Kastoria. My aunt Katerina was then working as a volunteer, where they met. She later on told me that, when she found out that he had served previously in Makronisos she asked. him if he had met or heard of me. When he replied that he knew me and that I was assigned to his company she sternly told him that he and the rest of the officers who had custody of me should be ashamed for the manner that they handled my issue. He profusely apologized to her for his inaction on my behalf, and for not believing in my insistence that I was innocent.

A middle aged mild mannered man from the eastern part of Macedonia, whose exact name could not recall, filled his vacancy in our company. He too called me at night to his office. Now after having so many previous visits I went in with no fear. After we went over all the same issues, I finally pleaded also with him to obtain from the police in Kastoria and from anywhere else the documents with the charges against me. Then I said again that if I am proven guilty of being involved with the EAM or communist party I would accept any form of punishment that he wished.

THE VOYAGE OF A SHEPHERD BOY

A couple of months passed and again I was called in but this time to my surprise, I was treated in a friendly manner. After some irrelevant comments he told me that he received response to his inquiry, and that the only comments in my file was that my family and I knew and occasionally spoke a dialect of the Slavic languages, which was known and spoken in all areas of the northern and northwestern borders of Greece. Then not being able to restrain myself, with some anger and sarcasm, I told him that indeed this is a crime, which justifies my exile here for about eleven months. Incidentally, two of my cousins, one a major of the elite forces of the Greek army and the other a major and surgeon in the largest hospital in Athens as well as two senators from our area knew and spoke that language. Perhaps they too should be sent to exile. Somewhat embarrassed and perhaps angered, he expressed his regrets and allowed me to go.

During all the eleven months up to that time my daily routine, as that of the rest of the soldiers was rising at dawn, then breakfast, to be followed by a morning formal report. Then, except on Sundays, we were divided in groups and under police supervision each group was taken to some form of manual work; cleaning the campus, carrying barrels of water to the company of the elite guard and the army police, building walls or bunkers or various signs at the top of the slope of the mountain and coloring them with asbestos, or clearing bushes and stones from unutilized areas for possible future use.

The aim obviously was to keep us constantly occupied with work no matter what the temperature was. At noon after lunch and a short rest period back to work until sunset. Supper at dusk followed by another formal report and then dismissal to our tents for the night. After dark a strict curfew was imposed. Only the army policemen were allowed to roam around the campus, whose footsteps I always dreaded. This daily routine was very often interrupted with a noon lecture of "enlightment" delivered by the director of the battalion's intelligence and resolution and restoration office, which was transmitted by the loudspeakers throughout all the campus of the battalion.

Nevertheless, after my last visit to the captain's office my occupational work miraculously improved. Every working day instead of going, as previously, to do manual work, I was ordered to go to the management office. There under the shade of the tent, instead of the burning sun, I helped with the inventory.

About two months later the captains of all three companies were asked by the major to send ten men each to his office. Our captain chose to send me also along with nine other men from our company. We all met in front of the major's tent. His aid came out and asked us to write a sentence, our name and our company's name on a piece of paper. I do not know why but I wrote "uden agathoteron tis ilikrinias," meaning nothing is more virtuous than candor. A few minutes later the aid collected the papers and dismissed us.

Some time later, to my great surprise, my captain called me and gave me my travel warrant and told me to pick up my belongings and be at the harbor in an hour to leave for Athens. Greatly surprised, I saluted him, and at in no time I was at the harbor. There twelve of us, four men from each company we were met by a young second lieutenant. He introduced himself and told us that we would all go for a month to Athens.

I could not believe what was happening. I was happy because I was leaving, even for a month from this Godforsaken island but also fearful too. I feared what the results of my medical school entrance examination had been. Since I was drafted and imprisoned I had always been thinking and worried about the results but the events, which took place since I left Thessaloniki, had not permitted me to make an inquiry as to whether I was accepted in the medical school. Now, finally, I would have the chance to find out but again I feared the answer.

A couple of days after we settled in Athens, with my heart pounding and my mouth dry from my anxiety, I called the dean's office in Thessaloniki. After I identified myself, I told the secretary that in 1947, immediately after the entrance examination, I was drafted in the armed forces and I had not heard about the results. Hearing, that all along I was in the army,

THE VOYAGE OF A SHEPHERD BOY

he immediately checked the records and pleasantly told me that I had been accepted in the medical school and that they had tried unsuccessfully to inform me. With a choked voice I thanked him and asked what I needed to do from then until my release from the service. He kindly replied, stay healthy and whenever you are ready come and enroll. It had been a long time since I had experienced such a great happiness and optimism. The last time was when I took the entrance examination for high school. This event made my stay in Athens most enjoyable and even the prospect of my return in a month to Makronisos was acceptable.

A week before our return to Makronisos I was asked to go to 415-Army Tuberculosis hospital to help them with the bookkeeping of the office of management. They indeed needed help badly because their books were in disarray. Although during that week I was able to finish most of the critical organization, both the director of the office of management, Mr. Diamantis Tsekouras, and the director of the hospital, Dr. Velios, were so pleased that they asked me if I would like to postpone my upcoming return to the Island Markonisos. Of course I agreed!

The director of the hospital was a career armed forces physician specializing in tuberculosis, in his fifties with the rank of major. During his long tenure he apparently had served for many years as a physician of the Scholi Evelpidon, an equivalent to our West Point and, as a result, he had great connections and influence in the army.

After a telephone call to the central office of the army he was granted the permission to keep me as long as he needed me. I was told that this decision was transmitted to my major in Makronisos and that I would be staying at the hospital until I was released from the army. After we had put all the office work in order my regular working hours were only until one o'clock pm and afterwards at my discretion any other time I felt I was needed.

Then for the first time since I left Thessaloniki I began to plan for my future. I found a bookkeeping job starting at two o'clock pm and lasting as long as I was needed. This extra work provided me a minor income that I saved for the days after my release from the service. I also bought the book of Physics, which is taught in the first medical school year and began to study whenever I had leisure time even though I did not know when and how I would start my medical studies. My living quarters, my food and my whole life in Athens was better than I could ever have dreamed (Figure 6).

Figure 6
In Athens while serving at the 415 Tuberculosis Hospital

Unfortunately, every month or so though this tranquility was disrupted by a telex sent from the major of my battalion in Makronisos to the hospital director ordering my immediate return to the island. Every time such an order was received it was relayed to the central office of the army where a request for permission to allow me to continue my stay in the hospital was granted.

This scenario continued for about seven months. Then one day in November a lieutenant and two soldiers from the company which guarded my battalion in Makronisos came early in the morning to the hospital and told me that they had orders from the major to arrest me and take me back immediately. I told them that I am certainly obeying the order but I had to delay my departure until the Director arrived, which would not be too long, so I could give him the keys of the offices, etc.

Finding me under guard, the Director asked what the matter was. The lieutenant apologized for the intrusion and showed him his orders. Obviously mad, the Director told them that they could take me now but it would not be for too long. Under guard I boarded their truck for the Port Sounion.

At our arrival there the lieutenant escorting me was shown an order from the central army office to release me to go back to the hospital. Somewhat puzzled he allowed me to leave. When I returned to the hospital both the director of the management office and the director of the hospital told me that in four days they would formally release me and allow me to go back to the island as a free soldier and not as a prisoner. They also added that shortly afterwards I would be transferred to an active unit in northern Greece and then in three to four months, I would be released from the army.

About three months earlier all the hostilities in our country finally had stopped. The Civil War was over, the Andartes were defeated, and our countrymen at last at peace, began the painful process of recovery and healing. The terror and destruction, which for such a long time was tearing our country to pieces, was replaced with peace and hope. The reduction of the army had begun and the older soldiers were already released, including my brother John allowed to return home and begin to rebuild their lives from the ashes that were left from the terrible civil war.

With these welcome developments and the information that in about four months I too would be released I returned to Makronisos full of hope and confidence that I too would soon start rebuilding my life.

When I was returning, from the Port of Sounion I faced the island and I saw this time not what I was seeing before, a wasteland and a land full of misery and torture, but a place from where my new pleasant journey would begin. Unfortunately, however, the second day of my return when the daily battalion order was read, the loud speaker announced that I was to be imprisoned for twenty days because I used "legitimate and illegitimate" means to stay in Athens, despite the Major's repeated orders to return.

I was astonished and could not believe my ears when I heard the news. What an irony I thought! I returned with hope and confidence that this would be a starting point towards a free life and not for a life of double confinement. How was it possible for my major to believe that I, an insignificant soldier, could control my stay in Athens? I was told at the hospital that the arrangement for my stay there was made through the higher army office, and that my major had been appropriately notified about these facts. Having confidence, however, in my superiors at the hospital, I was not terribly disturbed. I believed that soon they would arrange, as I was told, for my transfer from Makronisos to an active unit elsewhere. In addition I thought placing me in isolation would be beneficial to me since I would have plenty of time to read.

Eventually, under guard, I was taken to the prison, which was an area about fifty by fifty feet surrounded by barbwire, with a small tent in the center. I was only permitted to exit it under guard and usually to visit the bathroom. I passed my time alone reading and sometimes joking with the guard. A few days later, unexpectedly, a first lieutenant from the guard unit came and ordered me to immediately return with my belongings to my company.

My company's captain was still the man who several months earlier had made the inquiry as to why I was sent into exile. He gave me two weeks travel to another company, warrant for travel and furlough time and said, "You must have strong strings in Athens that are pulling for you." I told him that I did not know anyone except for the two officers at the hospital for whom I worked. His reply was, "it does not matter who is behind you. You deserve a break." His last statement greatly elevated my mood. I saluted him and he in turn wished me good luck.

February 11, 1950, leaving from the Port of Sounion, I looked toward the island once more with a great sense of relief, but also with the memory of all my trials and tribulations there.

Upon arriving to Athens, I visited the hospital. Both the director of the management office and the director of the hospital were pleased that I was now completely free. I did not inquire as to how my transfer happened, since I was fairly certain that they, through their connections at the central army office had arranged it. I thanked them for their trust in me and for all the help that they extended to me, and they in return wished me the best for my future. Subsequently, and periodically, we continued to correspond even after my immigration to America. I visited them again on two occasions, once during my senior year in medical school, and once during my first visit back to Greece seven years later. Both visits were cordial and fulfilling.

The unit to which I was transferred was stationed very near the territory of my village. In order to reach it I had to transverse longitudinally my country, which gave me the opportunity to see all the changes all the way from its bottom to its top. My trip in an open army truck was a sobering and depressing experience. The whole country was in ruins. All the villages and even some of the small towns were partially or completely destroyed. I saw house after house with only bare walls partially or completely intact. These cracked walls stood everywhere as if they were extending their arms in prayer for help. Most of the trees were cut or burned and most of the fields were uncultivated and wild. Only the bullet-ridden bunkers and the trenches stood fresh but even some of them were badly mangled.

My first stop after leaving Athens was the city of Thessaloniki. There I visited both my medical school and the teacher's academy. The administration of both schools then told me that the government recently enacted a special law concerning all students returning from the armed forces. It directed all schools of higher education to allow and facilitate those students who desired and were able to accelerate their study, even passing the courses of two academic years in a one-year period. It also provided that upon our release from the service we be allowed to start our school attendance even at the middle of the academic year. This gave me a glimmer of hope, that although there were no financial means in sight to support myself while attending in school, I might be able to find some way to continue my education after all.

Then after I went to Kastoria my hometown where I went to high school. The barbwire fences and the trenches at the neck of the peninsula and the machine gun bunkers staring from every prominent spot were a grim reminder of the recent past for these most unfortunate and distressing years of our civil war. However, seeing once more the smiling faces of the young and old citizens promenading in the main street, the bustling noise of the market with the white swans in the background swimming gracefully in the quiet lake, inspired relief and great hope.

My aunt Katrina and her family were happy to see me and learn that at last I had been exonerated and I was back in the regular armed forces. There I officially learned as to what happened to our village. Most of the young males and females, who had joined the Andartes, voluntarily or by force, had perished. Those who survived, and the rest of the population of our village, young and old, including my parents and the rest of our family, were taken to various communist countries, behind the iron curtain.

After I had finished my furlough travel privileges I reported to my new unit, 567 Infantry Battalion. It was stationed in a charming village, Andartico, nestled in the mountain Vitsi, close to the Yugoslavian border. Here after two years of service

I was finally given again a rifle. However, fortunately, since all the hostilities had ceased, I did not have to use it, and since I was again assigned to the office of management I did not have to learn how to use it. Less than two months later March 23, 1950, as I had been told in Athens, orders came for my release from the service.

3. RETURN TO MY VILLAGE

I picked up my certificate of discharge as well as my new travel warrant and with apprehension mixed with optimism, I began a new chapter of my life. Before I left this mountainous part of my country though I wanted to visit our farm and village and see what if anything, had remained. I got in an army vehicle, which was going to Kastoria, and after about twenty minutes of travel we arrived at our farm area. Most of the snow in the low elevations and in our farm area had just melted whereas farther up the mountains were still covered with a blanket of snow. I stepped off the vehicle, stood there for a while and looked around in disbelief. Nothing was even remotely close to what it was when I left two and a half years ago. Everywhere there was destruction and dissolution. The farmhouse, the stockyard, and the barns were all burned. The abundant green forests were demolished. All the trees were burned or cut and only black or brown stumps were poking out of the snow. The familiar sounds of the bells of our livestock and the barking of our dogs could not be heard. Everywhere deathly silence reined which was only occasionally disturbed by the sound of a jackdaw. The cornfields, the wheat fields and the vegetable gardens, instead of being meticulously cultivated, lay dormant as if they were begging for the care of the pre-war era. As I was entering our fields, in a ditch next to a patch of snow I came upon the scattered remains of some clothes, a pair of old shoes and bones including a human skull. I spontaneously whispered "eonia sou i mnimi", may your memory be eternal, no matter who you were and why you were there. From his clothing and his teeth it appeared that perhaps he was a young male possibly killed during the last hostilities.

Solemnly I walked to the site of our stockyard. I sat on a rock, the most prominent spot above this area and I aimlessly scouted with my eyes all our area trying to erase what I had just seen and trying to relive all the pleasant moments that I had spent there during my childhood. From this spot I walked the familiar road to our village.

As I face it, its view was harrowing. The only buildings standing were the church and a handful of houses including ours. The forest, which spread from just above the village and over the slope of the mountains, was gone. The atmosphere here, as everywhere else, was deadly quiet. No voices of happy children playing in the square or the schoolyard could be heard and there was no living creature anywhere.

Walking from house to house was like walking from one eviscerated corpse to another with part of its remains scattered in the yards or the streets. Our house although standing was completely skeletized. There were no floors, windows, doors or stairs and nothing from our belongings could be found. Everything was taken away. Our hidden underground storage room had been found, looted and left open. There were big gaps everywhere in the ground inside and outside of the house, which had been dug in order to find any valuables that were hidden. The whole picture was devastating, angering and unbelievable. Who were these animals that came and looted what had been left? How could they possibly profit from the things that they stole during or in the aftermath of our national calamity? Sad and disgusted I walked to Kastoria.

VI. UNIVERSITY YEARS

During the last months in the army I began to think what I would do after my discharge. All of my family except for my brother John was gone, and all our tangible assets had been destroyed. John was released from the army shortly after the end of the war and had found work and settled in Athens. The only possessions that I had were my army uniform and a very small amount of money that I had saved from my extra work while I was in Athens. I therefore thought, since more than half of the academic year was already gone, it will be prudent for me to go to Athens and join my brother and work somewhere until the new academic year began.

During my short visit with him we reminisced about the past, discussed our present situation and looked toward our future. He told me that he had secured a difficult but stable job, and that he was in process of securing a visa to immigrate to America. He then asked me about my plans. I told him, that although the newly enacted law allowed me to start my studies immediately, I thought it would be prudent for me to stay here and work for the remaining academic year, save some money if possible and then in about six months when the new academic year began to reassess my situation and make a decision. He then emphatically said, no, you are going immediately to start your studies, and then jointly as we go along we will find solutions for all our challenges.

His unconditional offer of support overwhelmed me. I knew too that his only possession was his army uniform, but despite this his conviction that I should go on was what I needed to overcome my fears and to start my new uncharted road. The next evening he took me to the railroad station, squeezed some money in my hand and we again parted. With my heart flooded with gratitude we waved to each other as the train pulled out of the station.

Inside I sat on a wooden bench. As the outside images flashed before my eyes, so did a myriad of concerns went through my mind about my future, and more immediately about where I would be going in the morning when I stepped off the train.

The only individual that I knew in Thessaloniki was my cousin Argyri Paragyriou who was a student in the university. I decided to visit him and get his opinion concerning my lodgings. He was renting a room in an apartment house on Aristotelous Square. I arrived in Thessaloniki early in the morning. Almost everybody was up and rushing to work. I walked to my cousin's place passing by the familiar bustling market place.

His room was on the first floor of an apartment house. It had one bed, a small desk, a bench and one window facing the back walls of the adjacent apartment houses.

My cousin too was in the armed forces and had been released about five months earlier. He was a junior in the agriculture school and in a few weeks he would be finishing the theoretical courses and he then would go to the university farm for the practical courses until October when the new academic year began.

After we went over our experiences during the past almost three years, he asked me what I was planning to do next. I told him that I would like to enroll in both the medical school and the teacher's academy and I would try to get as many credits as I could during the remaining three and a half months of the academic year. First however, I had to find shelter and I asked him for any suggestions. He generously offered for me to stay with him, use the bench for sleeping for the next three weeks, and then after that I could have all the room to myself until October. This way he said I did not have to worry about rents, etc. and I could keep the room occupied so the landlords would not take it for him and rent it for a better price.

Now that my lodging issue had been solved the next day I enrolled for the first year courses for both schools. Because of time constraints, though I attended only those lectures, which required attendance, also, the entire lab work required by the teacher's academy and the physics lab work in the medical school. Having done that, I was given the privilege of having two meals, breakfast and lunch, which were given free by both schools to students in need. I postponed the lab work for the remaining two subjects of the first year of medical school until the first trimester of the new academic year.

As I have mentioned earlier the special law enacted for the students who were drafted during the civil war allowed us to take the final examinations on each subject in medical school, sequentially, provided we had completed the attendance for the required lecture and lab work.

By the end of June I had completed all the required courses for the teacher's academy, taken the final examinations, and I was promoted to its second and senior year. I also completed the required lecture attendance and the laboratory work for physics.

My cousin Argyri finished his required courses as he planned, and went on to the university farm. Now alone, undisturbed by anyone except for my own thoughts I devoted all my time studying physics. It was a hot summer. There were no means of cooling the room and no breeze could reach the window because of the surrounding buildings. I studied in the room until noon while the temperature was still tolerable and in the afternoon I went to the library. At night before bed I would usually, aimlessly walk along the harbor of the bustling city of Thessaloniki. The lightened white houses and buildings of the city were displayed in a semicircular manner on the slope of the surrounding hill from almost its top down to the seashore. These images were reflected in the calm waters of the gulf. Seeing these lights and hearing the lapping of the waves at the coast provided me the mental and emotional relief that I badly needed.

In October I passed the examination on physics. This accomplishment, in addition to greatly lifting my spirit, made me eligible for housing in the only one student dormitory that the university had then.

Figure 7
The Beloved student's house.

The mission of the dormitory, the student's house, as it was called, was to provide complete shelter free of charge to the students who had meager or no financial resources, and who also had good academic standing. It was a beautiful neoclassical building of gray white color with big windows, two sizable balconies one on the second and the third floors facing the front of the house, and a small balcony on the second floor overhanging the narrow cobble stone street (Figure 7). All the windows, as well as the doors leading to the balconies, had shutters stained green. The floor of its basement was covered with cement and on one side there were five showerheads lined up next to each other for all the students to use. The other side we used to occasionally cook a scratch meal, on a primus stove. On the first floor there were four large bedrooms with four beds in each room. On the eastern side between the bedrooms there was a small room with a desk and a chair for the director of the house and on the western side between the two bedrooms there was a corridor leading to the restrooms. In the center of the floor there was a large living room like area. The second floor was identical to the first floor except for a small room with a single bed, which was sitting just above the director's office. In the area just above the bathrooms of the first floor, there was a terrace and bathrooms. The third floor had only one large room with a door leading to a balcony and to a terrace. In this room there were three long tables placed in a Π shape with many wooden chairs lined up around all sides of the tables. All the students used this room exclusively for studying. The house had no other facilities for cooling except for the breeze through the balcony doors and the large windows. The only heated areas were the two living room areas and the studying room. In each of them there was a wood-burning stove. In front of the house there was a sizable yard surrounded with six foot tall stonewalls and a thick wooden gate of equal height. This area was used as a flower garden, cultivated and cared for by the students. The house sheltered thirty-three students, four in each of the eight large bedrooms and one in the small room on the second floor.

 In October, as soon as I met the criteria to stay in the student's house, I moved in. The single bed in the small room on the second floor was assigned to me. The room had a bed, a small head table and room enough for one person to turn around. This room, since I was using it only for sleeping could not have been better for me. As it turned out, it was my permanent shelter until I left for the United States.

Having now secured permanent free housing and two free meals each day, I felt, relatively secure. My army clothes would undoubtly last for a long time and my supper could be made very frugal consisting of bread, cheese, and pasta. Therefore, I could now center all my attention and effort on my courses.

Fortunately, my living environment within our house was very conducive to learning. The men sheltered in the house represented all the branches of the university; the schools of law, physics, philosophy, philology, theology, medicine, etc. They were 24 to 30 years of age and all of them had the same aim, to do well in the courses and graduate as soon as possible. They were self-disciplined, overly motivated, kind, respectful and supportive of each other. In essence we were one big family.

Our house was full of vitality. Every school day early in the morning, Monday through Friday every one of us would get up and rush to the student's club for breakfast and then disperse to our respective lectures, to our lab work, to the library or to our study room. Lunch at the student's club was followed by a short period of rest, and then we went back to our busy schedules. In the evening most of us would be in the study room until late into the night. During the reading hours all areas around the study room were kept quiet. On Saturday morning most of us would come out in our flower garden to work for a while, digging, planting, fertilizing, pruning, watering, and weeding. As a result, all of our flowers were thriving and our garden was the envy of everyone who passed by. On Sunday morning, most of us would line up to take a shower while some of us would wash our clothes while showering. Saturday and Sunday afternoons consisted of studying for those of us who had a heavy load interspersed with a game, a song, or sometimes just joking and socializing.

My daily routine was, as was the routine of all the students in the house, attending the required lectures and laboratory work and studying all year round.

One of my main diversions was going to the seaside for a walk or for a chess game with one of my two friends, Filipa Karamata or more often Theochari Karavida. Both were medical students, cohabitants and both had graduated from the high school of Kastoria. I would also occasionally visit my cousin Argyri while he was in Thessaloniki, or his friend Kosta Boukouvala who subsequently became my friend and still is to this day.

Another diversion was going occasionally for supper to a most hospitable restaurant, which offered good food, had very reasonable prices and whose customers were university students many of them with limited or practically no funds. It was owned and operated by uncle Vangellis, as all of us used to call him, and his wife. Uncle Vangellis was a short, overweight, middle-aged man, kind, generous, and trusting. His trust and generosity towards the students who everyday crowded his place was unimaginable. Not infrequently some of the students, including myself, would not have any money or not enough to pay for the meal. On such an occasion, before the meal we would inform him about that fact. Invariably his answer was "sit down, eat and pay me whenever you can". At the end of the meal he would write on a scrap of paper the amount owed and give us the paper. To my knowledge he did not keep records of who did or did not pay and how much each owed. He was totally dependent for his reimbursement upon the student's integrity and I am confident that nobody let him down. He had no children of his own but he used to say that he had more children than anybody else and that we were his children, the university students who crowed in his restaurant every day. I was and still am thankful for the trust and kindness that he extended to me whenever I needed help.

I visited him on three different occasions since I immigrated to America. On the third occasion I was sad to find out that he had passed on, but I was confident that he had gone to paradise where he deserved to be. The previous two visits were cordial and emotional. He appeared to be proud and most appreciative of my visits.

Other memorable diversions during the university years included two visits to my aunt Katerina in Kastoria. The first was during Christmas holidays while I was a third year medical student and the second during Easter holidays in my senior year. Thankfully the landscape everywhere then had changed tremendously since wartime. As our bus was tranversing the valleys, ascending and descending the hills and mountains to reach its destination, everything around us was tranquil, relatively rehabilitated, vivacious and beautiful.

There were no more restrictions as to which road to travel, no more destruction of everything as before and, above, all no thoughts of uncertainty and desperation for me. Having peace and tranquility in our country, and most importantly, having fulfilled one of my goals by graduating from the teacher's academy and also being on the road or close to the finish line towards to fulfill my second and main goal to graduate from medical school despite all the adversities made me very happy. The six-hour road trip was most pleasant.

While I was there my aunt's hospitality made those holidays very memorable. I was and am most grateful and indebted to my aunt and her family who made these days so pleasant and for the hospitality, care and support they afforded me during all the previous years.

In October 1950 after I settled in the student's home, I enrolled in all the courses of the senior year of the teacher's academy, and for the lab work of the remaining subjects of the first year of medical school. In January 1951 I passed the final examinations of these subjects and enrolled in the second year of medical school, attending all the lectures in anatomy some in physiology almost none in organic chemistry and also doing the entire lab work for all three subjects (Figure 8). I was fortunate that all the lectures and lab works of the teacher's academy were in the morning hours and those of the medical school were in the after noon so that I could hop from one to the other and meet the requirements of all the courses in which I had enrolled.

THE VOYAGE OF A SHEPHERD BOY

Figure 8
Cadaver dissection during the anatomy course.

In June I had targeted a plan to give the final examination in all of the teacher's academy courses and also take the final examination in anatomy and then defer my other subjects for the autumn period.

The final examination in anatomy started before the finals for the teacher's academy. It was given by the professor, orally, two students at a time and in alphabetical order. The examinations lasted several days. Because of the high failure rate, as the examinations progressed, some of the students decided not take them at that time and deferred them for the next examining period. Once I discovered, this deferment by some students, in order to prevent a possible conflict between my examinations in anatomy with the final examination of the teacher's academy, I asked the professor if he could examine me during any of the idle periods that he might have. Somewhat surprised, with my rush to be examined while some of my classmates refused to appear, he told me to come the next day and at the first opportunity that he had, he would take me.

The professor of anatomy, Dr. Savas, was a short man in his fifties, very strict but an excellent teacher. All his lectures were instructive and clear and all of them were excellently illustrated by his own colored drawings on the blackboard. They were so vivid, clear and so impressive that during my examinations I could clearly project them in front of me. Despite the rumors that he was a terror, when I was examined I found him stern but relatively pleasant. I answered all his questions and I left his office, elated.

By then it was dark outside where three of my curious classmates were waiting to hear about the examinations and what questions I was asked. We walked from there to the nearest streetcar stop. The street was overcrowded with people taking the usual evening promenade.

As we were walking and I was very exuberant, and perhaps too loud describing my examination, I heard a voice from behind us calling my name. I turned around and unexpectedly I saw the director of the teacher's academy with his wife and his teenage son. He called me to join them and asked me somewhat perplexed, what I was doing in that neighborhood. It was obvious that he had heard our discussions. With a trembling voice I told him that I had just finished my final examination in anatomy. It seems that you did well he said. I reluctantly agreed with him and I was asked to see him the next day in his office. I was stunned. All my joy was killed. I knew then that the next day I had to explain my dishonesty concerning my original high school diploma, when four years earlier I applied for the entrance examinations. I also feared because of my dishonesty I might be expelled, at least from the teacher's academy. I went to my room shaken, thinking that tomorrow all my efforts might be shattered. I could not sleep all night. The next day frightened, I met with the director, Mr. Papanastasiou. He was an imposing but friendly, kind man. Obviously angered he asked me what is going on. I thought then I had better spill out everything. Our conversation progressed as follows; I told him that my desire always was to become a physician. The ravages of the war forced me to consider the teaching profession because of its shorter studying period, and as result it was more within my reach. I told him that all our possessions were destroyed during the war. I had no means to support myself. These facts forced me to be untruthful to his institution and with a heavy heart I had to state that my original high school diploma was destroyed during the war. I had to choose then to either abandon my plans or to make a false statement. Then with tearful eyes I said I was sorry for the statement that I made then, under duress.

As he listened to my explanation, the anger in his face dissipated and he said it is unfortunate because he was planning to send me with a scholarship to Paris for further studies. However, he said, that although he could not condone the lie, and according to the law he should expel me from the school, he could see that my intent was not to hurt the society but to help it. Therefore, he commended me for my draconian efforts to attain what I wanted and he said I had his blessings and confidence in my success. He then invited me to take the final examinations and to get my degree so that I might perhaps use it in the future. I thanked him, and reduced almost to zero emotionally, I left full of gratitude and admiration. In the next few days, I took the finals and he personally handed me my degree.

Afterwards, unfortunately I had only one indirect contact with him and that was a few days after my graduation from medical school. At that time he issued, to my great surprise, a congratulatory note in my honor in the local newspaper.

After graduation from the teacher's academy, however, I did not pursue teaching to attain some financial recovery. Instead, I felt the need to continue the momentum to graduate from medical school, which was now attainable. My lodging and two meals were still secured. My cousin Agryri, after graduating from agricultural school and shedding his student status, graciously gave me his nice suit, and his shoes (Figure 9). Now, since the army uniform was worn I had another respectable outfit to wear for special occasions. Also, in the meantime, my brother John had immigrated to the United States and found a job on a farm, as many of the current migrants do. As soon as he secured an income he started to share a fraction of it with me. Although nominally it was small, in substance it was very large, since it was spared from his meager income. This small financial but great physiological support in conjunction with everything else gave me the security to concentrate on my medical school courses.

Figure 9
Photo with my brother John before he left for America.

As I went along, I finished them one after the other pleasantly and uneventfully until my fourth year into medical school. Then in January when I went to enroll in the course of pathologic anatomy (pathology), the secretary told me that the professor does not allow her to do that because the course started in October. I responded that I was aware that the lectures were going on for three months but the special law of the government gives us, who have served in the armed forces, the right to enroll even in the middle of the courses. She replied that she would check again with the professor and let me know. When I revisited her, she apologetically said that the professor refused to accept me. I then asked her if I could speak to him personally. With his consent she led me to his offices.

THE VOYAGE OF A SHEPHERD BOY

The professor, Dr. Iliakis, was in his fifties, an imposing and over confident figure that was feared by all the students. He was portrayed as a stubborn, mean spirited individual particularly towards those who challenged him. The prevailing view among the students was that whoever got on unfavorable terms with him would take a long time to pass his examinations. As I sat opposite to him, he asked me what I wanted. I told him that I had just completed all the requirements of the third medical school year, I had enrolled in the other fourth year courses and I wanted to enroll in his course. His answer was that he could not do it because a third of his lectures were over. I replied that I knew that but the law allowed me to enroll in the middle of any course. His answer was that he could not do it because he was concerned as to the standards of medical education when I so drastically shortened the courses. But I replied I could not waste ten months doing nothing until the new academic year. He said he could not believe that I was unhappy since I had finished early the third year courses while he had a son in the University of Paris who had to repeat his last year's course.

Angered because of his answer and desperate because I saw that he did not intend to change his mind, I unconsciously and unwisely slapped my hand on his desk and told him that his son had to repeat the course because most likely he did not fulfill the requirements and I had nothing to do for the next ten months. Furious, I left his office. Nevertheless, one week later the secretary informed me that I was allowed to take his course. I was told that he had changed his mind after he checked my academic and non-academic status. From then on, until June, I was his target. He always checked whether or not I was present in his lectures and occasionally checked whether or not I had paid attention.

Because of this negative attention and because of his overall reputation, all my classmates myself included, feared that it would take me a long time before I passed his final examinations. His examinations were oral with six students at a time. In June, late in the afternoon six students, including me were waiting outside of the professor's office for our final examination. All of us we were frightened, myself because I had challenged him previously, and my classmates because they feared that his anger and revenge towards me might affect them as well. In order to minimize such a thing I told them that I would sit at the end of the line so that by the time it was my turn to be questioned, he would have finished and graded them. Upon entering his office I did not notice any change in his facial expression, which was an encouraging sign to me. We sat in the order we had agreed upon. His routine was that if a question was not answered it was passed to the next student and the next until the correct answer was given. In the course of the examinations several unanswered questions of my classmates came to me. I was fortunate enough to answer all of them. He was obviously pleased with my performance and when my turn for direct questioning came, to my surprise he said, I would ask you only one question before we finish. Although by then I was feeling very good and most of my fears were gone when I heard that I would be asked only one question I thought that it would be like the kiss of death. He asked me a somewhat esoteric question which I answered with no hesitation. He appeared pleased and even cracked a smile in the corner of his mouth. Contrary to my previous fears as well as my classmates not only did he pass me, but he gave me an excellent grade.

He was unfair because of his unwillingness to enroll me in his course, but certainly he was fair and just in his examinations and grading. From then on it appeared that instead of being his target I was one of his favorites. I had two additional courses with him, one in the fifth year of medical school and one on my senior year. Both of them were uneventful and enjoyable.

Over gratified I left his office and went directly to our studying room. Since all the students, including myself, we were expecting my examinations to be a disaster everybody was curious to hear how everything went. They were surprised and happy to hear that my examination went well and perhaps this outcome modified their opinion of the professor, as it did mine.

However, because the next day I had final examinations on another big subject (nosiology), internal medicine, there

THE VOYAGE OF A SHEPHERD BOY

was no time for celebration. I tried to review the material as much as possible that night, and the next morning I walked to Kendriko hospital where the examinations were given. The professor of internal medicine, Dr. Deligiannis was a mild mannered, impeccably well dressed man. His examinations were conducted by drawing a raffle ticket. He, or most likely his aids, had written each of the internal medicine topics on a scratch piece of paper, which was folded and placed in a basket.

As soon as I was seated he shook the basket and asked me to pick my first lot, to open it, and to answer the question. This was repeated three times. There was no other interaction with him except of his facial expressions each time I gave the answer. The question on my third and last lot was about a rare disease, Tsutsungamushi, which is encountered in oriental countries. In the professor's textbook it was described in fine print at the bottom of the page. Fortunately, perhaps because of its odd name, or the unusual site where it was described in his textbook, it had drawn my attention. As a result I was able to describe it easily. Then his face lightened up, he thanked me and dismissed me. It was obvious that I had done well.

I walked the hospital corridors with uncontainable happiness. Having passed within 24 hours the two major subjects one of which neither myself nor anybody else was expecting me to pass created an overflow of adrenaline which gave me a sense of floating rather than stepping on the ground as well as an indescribable euphoria. In the hall of the student's house I met my friend Theochari who also had scored success in his examinations. Both of us, full of joy and unrestrained energy, left the house and walked endlessly from place to place in the city, talking constantly who knows what. Finally, we settled for an early good supper at Vangellis' restaurant and returned to the student's house to share our happiness with the rest of the students.

The next two academic years passed relatively easy, generating constant optimism and happiness. Everyday the light at the end of the tunnel was getting closer and brighter.

As a result no matter what obstacles appeared as I was dashing towards the finish line, they could not block me.

In June 1954, my target plan was to pass the final examinations of all the courses of the senior year and graduate. As a result the day before the final examinations on the last subject my anxiety peaked, which perhaps caused me a severe hiccup, which could not be abolished with any conventional or unconventional remedy. I could get no rest or sleep, let alone study. Exhausted from it, I appeared for the final examinations. Miraculously just as the first question was given, the hiccup stopped. It was the magic drug that I needed.

A week later July 10, 1954, all the graduates dressed in our finest gathered in front of the administration building of the university. Before the graduation date, I had reluctantly asked my friend Kostas who was a tailor if he would make my first suit since I had left my village. He generously agreed with the provision that I would pay him as soon as I started working. He alone owned and operated a small men's shop. We picked out the material from the several samples that he had and in a few days he had it ready.

After we gave the Hippocratic Oath, we all lined up on the marble steps of the university's administration building for the group picture (Figure 10). Then I solemnly walked out of the university yard turned around and glanced through the iron railing once more at the neo-classical building and with my diploma in my hand I slowly, walked towards the student's house full of emotions. I was happy and proud, on one hand, because at last did I not only fulfill my dream and became a physician but I accomplished it in almost four years instead of six years. I was wondering and worrying on the other hand as to whether I would be able to meet the terms of the oath that I had just given.

Figure 10
Medical class picture at our graduation

I walked to the student's house where a few of the students who had not left for the summer and who were my only family members, congratulated me warmly for the occasion. Not having anywhere else to go, I spent that summer, as I did all the previous ones, alone. Only the director of the house came during the day for a short period, and the rest of the day I was left to look after the house.

During my medical school years I could not conclusively decide which specialty I would pursue, as I presume many of the medical school students do today, although I knew that it would be a surgical one. The surgeon's direct, definitive and immediately revealing approach to each case greatly attracted me. Despite that presumption, since my remaining stay in Greece was short, I thought it would be prudent to pursue an internal medicine internship to strengthen my basic medical knowledge.

I was assigned to the public (Dimotiko) hospital. Each day I walked slowly the steep cobbled stone road, which led to it. Somehow I wanted to delay the testing of my ability to face my patients, to provide them their initial care and to assume responsibility for the outcome.

Although I thought that I did well during my medical school years, suddenly I felt intimidated and even frightened by the prospect of being first and solo caring for those who entrusted their well being and life to me. However, immediately after I walked in, I felt the knowledge that I had acquired was there ready for use. After a cursory review of the patient's records with the chief nurse by me, I checked each patient, and indicated to the nurse the course of their management. After my lengthy rounding, the Attending arrived for rounds. Now, the uncertainty and fear reappeared as to whether I had made the correct decisions for the patients' management, and whether he would approve.

The Attending was Dr. Vasilis Rousoulis, a gentle and polite man in his early fifties, an internist and one of the handfuls of cardiologists of that era. Contrary to the majority of the attendings who were ready to ridicule their residents for minimal errors or for a diversion from their thought process, he gently added his suggestions to the patients' management with the appropriate justification for each of them. It was evident that he believed that abuse, degradation, and the instilment of fear in his subordinates not only were not an effective way of teaching and learning, but it was a destructive one.

The six months of my internship tenure passed uneventfully for the most part, except for the usual frustrations of an internship and especially because of the limited support sometimes from some of the ancillary services.

In the late evening and night hours, one night this fact brought me to a boiling point. Before midnight a semi comatose girl was brought to our ward. According to her medical history she was diabetic. I immediately requested the conventional lab work but I was told that the laboratory was closed for the night, although the on call technician was sleeping in the hospital compound. When I demanded that she get up and run the tests she told the nurse that if I were a physician I should be able to treat the patient without the lab work. Agitated, I personally walked to her quarters and asked for her to get up and run the tests.

Then in the morning she could report to her superior and the hospital authorities that I was an incompetent physician since I demanded laboratory tests while I was treating a comatose diabetic patient. The next morning I reported the incidence to my attending who requested and obtained the needed changes as to the availability of laboratory support.

During the six months between my graduation and departure from Greece I enrolled for the first time in English language night courses. I tried to learn during that limited time as much as I could so that I would not be completely mute when I immigrated to my new country.

Although my earnings were very small still since I had free lodging, my life as a neophyte physician was pleasant. For the first time in over four years since I had lived in the city I tasted a little bit of its social life. It was indeed enjoyable but, as is natural, not free of worry.

Since my brother John immigrated to America I was very much looking forward to my new life in America. The destruction of our property, the dispersion of my family to all corners of the world had disrupted my roots in Greece. My admiration of the United States for all its values and its great advancements in the field of medicine had inspired in me a burning desire to follow my brother John who had already immigrated there.

Although I was, I am, and I would always be very proud of my motherland and love its people and lifestyle, I wanted to move permanently to America because of all the tragedies that I experienced during my life in Greece. Therefore in the midst of my senior medical school year I asked my brother John to make the appropriate invitation. In January 1955, the local American consulate notified me that my papers for immigration were ready. Then new emotions rose. I was happy because I would move to the land of freedom, progress, and opportunity, which was a close image of Greece during its golden period of Periklis about 2500 years ago. I was also distraught, worried and fearful because I was leaving a relatively secure environment that I had just established, and because I was uncertain of the future. These differing emotions in part caused my first and last alcohol intoxication during the farewell party, which was given for me by my student house friends. Indeed it was a wonderful and at the same time, a disagreeable experience.

PART B

VII. INTRODUCTION TO MY NEW COUNTRY

January 25, 1955, I packed my few belongings and left for the railroad station with an overflow of gratitude and indebtness to my university and my beautiful country for giving me the opportunity to fulfill my dreams. This accomplishment was possible because not only was I not required to pay tuition but I was also provided free shelter and two free meals throughout my study period.

It was sunset time. As the colors of the rainbow were displayed in the western horizon against the Greek blue sky, I boarded the oriental express train for Paris, sat on my wooden seat and stared at the sunset's colorful lights. As they faded behind the horizon so were fading away my last few minutes of being in my motherland.

The myriad of thoughts and the different and interesting scenes that rushed by my window one after the other, as well as the train's rapid speed made my long travel to Paris barely noticeable. I stayed in Paris six days waiting for my ship to arrive. With many thoughts parading through my mind, I roamed from place to place admiring the wonders of this enchanting city. The grace of the opera house, the grandeur of the Eiffel Tower, the majesty of the Louvre Museum, the colorful Montmart and the serene rolling of the Seine River made my stay there most enjoyable. I visited with my cousin Argyri who was then living there and we reminisced about our past with a mixture of sorrow and nostalgia. At the date of my departure Argyri generous and helpful as always, drove me to the Port of La Havre. There among numerous other boats stood, the giant ship, America. As I made my last step going from my old continent towards the new one, I waved and whispered to him, until our next meeting whenever that will be. Slowly then, through the crowded corridors I found my cabin. It was a small cubicle with a bunk bed and no outside view. My initial experience was one of claustrophobia. As I settled in my cabin it was already evening and everybody was invited for supper. The massive dining hall was a sea of humans, young and old. They were all dressed up and cheerful as if they were celebrating a new beginning. The food was abundant, more than I had ever seen before, with great variety but a little strange for my taste. I sampled as much as I could, and then walked from place to place trying to explore this new micropolis. It was an impressive experience; fancy bars, game rooms, swimming pools, were all over the place. All of them were crowded with people trying to saturate themselves with everything that was offered. After a while I returned to my cabin. My roommate was a young German man whose English and accent were as poor as mine. I tried to converse with him but we could not reasonably communicate. Somewhat disappointed and desperate, I turned to my dictionary and book to improve my English vocabulary.

In the morning I noticed that our ship, despite its size, was bouncing, suggesting that we were in the open and angry waters of the Atlantic. In the dining room and everywhere the crowd was thinner than the previous night and some of those that had come for breakfast were pale and unbalanced. As we progressed into our voyage the crowd everywhere became sparser and all the entertaining areas appeared somewhat deserted, giving the opportunity to those of us who were not seasick to freely enjoy all the facilities.

On the morning of the eighth day of our voyage, it was announced that we were almost at the Port of New York. It was a cold, lightly snowing, mid February day. I ran up to the deck, along with the rest of the travelers who were spared from being

THE VOYAGE OF A SHEPHERD BOY

seasick to have my first glance at my new country. The panoramic sight of New York City with the Statue of Liberty standing in front of the imposing skyscrapers behind it and enforcing its majesty was a breathtaking view. Despite the bitter, penetrating cold, we stood there in admiration until the ship anchored. I took my first step on the shore, overwhelmed with the feeling that I was taking the first step towards a future full of opportunity, challenges and responsibilities.

With my suitcase in hand I walked, along the way asking, in my rudimentary English, for directions to the central station. Although the cold was blistering my apprehension, excitement, and my fast pace made it almost unnoticeable.

I purchased my ticket, boarded the train to Detroit where my brother John lived and sat on the benches, next to a well-dressed black man with a shining watch chain across his chest. Not clearly understanding the conductor's announcements and fearing that I would miss my stop I tried to ask him to remind me when we had reached Detroit. After considerable efforts and frustration from both of us he assured me that he would let me know when we had reached my destination. Indeed, as we approached Detroit he kindly alerted me.

Stepping out of the train it was, as in New York, bitter cold with snow everywhere. I took a taxi to Forrest Street, the address that I had for my brother John. It was a middle class residential area with one-floor single-family houses lined up a short distance from each other. Each had a sizable yard between them and the road. Uninvited and unannounced, I knocked on the door and an unknown lady in her early forties appeared. I asked for my brother. With her kind, gentle smile, she said you must be Panagiotis. She knew from my brother John that I was on the way and I would be arriving at any time. She told me that my brother was not living there and that he should be at work. She warmly invited me in and went on to tell me that she was my Aunt Gloria who had immigrated to America from Greece when I was a youngster. Her house was of a moderate size, impeccably arranged, clean and carpeted which was a novelty for me. She offered me something to eat, as was customary of her and she made a myriad of inquiries about my trip, the old country and whether I had any news from my parents. She was a beautiful lady, green eyed and blond, as well as gentle, kind, caring and hospitable. In addition she was an excellent cook. Her homemade crispy old country bread, her various kinds of pitas and the variety of meals and desserts that she used to make were unsurpassable and craved by all who had tasted them. Her husband Basil Karstofsky was a kind, low-key, soft-spoken and hardworking man. They had two sons and a daughter Tina who was a mirror image of her mother. She was married to a joyful, warm, pleasant, and helpful man, Lincoln Naumoff, who had a great sense of humor and wit. He was a teacher and an accomplished musician. Both Uncle Basil and Aunt Gloria offered for me to stay with them until we had arranged my housing. Their generous and warm welcome made the first two days in my new country most enjoyable. I had many warm and pleasant visits and delicious meals with them over many years afterwards. In fact they always made me feel at home whenever I was with them. I am most thankful for the unlimited hospitality that they extended to me over many years.

Late on the first night of my arrival my brother John came to see me. The meeting was emotional, joyful and full of a sense of reward. Although the time of our separation chronologically was not too long, about four years, it had been interspersed with many interesting events in our lives, which we talked about for hours. He was as happy, proud, and relieved, as I was to see the successful end of the challenging journey that we had traveled. Just a few months previously he had moved from Minneapolis to Detroit, changed his job and was preparing the grounds to start his own business as a tailor. He was renting a room next to Wayne State University. Two days later, with the consent of his landlord, I moved in with him.

As yet I had made no arrangements for my medical training nor did I know what steps I needed to take to do so. Not having anything else to do and badly in need of improving my rudimentary English I enrolled in a one hour course in English three times per week at the university. In the meantime I unfortunately determined that to secure an internship position I should have applied to various institutions a long time before and that by now, which was mid March, all positions had been filled. Therefore in desperation, I first, contacted most of the Detroit hospitals for any openings and then I extended my radius of search to other cities. It was like walking blindfolded into unknown territory. Finally, in April I was offered a job at a hospital in Toledo, Ohio, with the provision that until July I would be working only in the outpatient clinic. I had to start working. Not having any other choices, I accepted the offer and moved there. The hospital was private, not affiliated with a university but with approved training programs.

Of course, coming to the new world everything was new and somehow strange to me. The territory around me seemed unending and the land flat, fertile and well cultivated. The city buildings were bigger, brighter and more modern than at home. The residential areas were spread out with single-family dwellings and large green lawns and with usually more than one private car parked in the driveway. The streets were wide enough to accommodate the great number of large cars. The food was abundant and somewhat strange to me, especially, the bread. Most closed spaces were somewhat foggy and smelling of tobacco. Young and old, males and females, had frequently a cigarette in their mouth or fingers. In the old country only adult males smoked and most of them relatively well to do financially. I wondered if this indiscriminate smoking was another manifestation of prosperity. Nevertheless, the hospital where I moved was impressive, large, more modern, clean, and orderly. However, contrary to my expectations its teaching program was not better than that I had left.

For the first couple months I showed up for work only in the outpatient clinics. Because of my limited English fluency, my first experience was shocking and difficult for me, as I am sure it was for the patients. Taking history and prescribing the management of the patients was an ordeal with my broken English and the patients' American accent, to which I was not exposed. Despite this barrier to my pleasant surprise, the patients were pleasant, appreciative and understanding.

Beginning July I started the duties of a rotating internship. As time progressed my communication skills appeared to be improving and I became accustomed to my new working environment. Everybody around me was polite, helpful, supportive, and appeared appreciative of my effort and work. My life was centered around the hospital. My free time was spent reading and occasionally visiting my relatives in Detroit.

Although everything was progressing smoothly I was still uneasy. I frequently missed my native country Greece, its people, its way of life, and its beautiful climate. However, most importantly I was concerned about my training. As I mentioned earlier the training program at the hospital, although approved, was not exactly what I had envisioned. Therefore, now that I had learned the steps I needed to take toward the search for a residency position at a university program, I began the process early, being aware that as a foreign graduate it would be a very difficult if not impossible task. I thought in order to have even a remote chance to find a position that I should write to all university training programs, a task that I did not feel that I would be able to do effectively by myself.

Fortunately, on one of my visits to Detroit I mentioned my dilemma to Lincoln Naumoff, my Aunt Gloria's son-in-law. Although up to that time I had limited contact with him, he not only generously offered to help me but he undertook the entire project and worked diligently with me. He found the addresses of all the university training programs, wrote all the required letters, and helped me to fill all the applications. He did all these tasks pleasantly and with the same zeal as if they were for him. I was and still am most appreciative for these efforts and especially for the friendship and hospitality that Lincoln and his wife Tina have given me over the last fifty years. Anytime I visited Detroit

THE VOYAGE OF A SHEPHERD BOY

during the subsequent years it has been a delight for me to visit with them, to enjoy their company and Tina's delicious meals.

Although I had very little hope finding a university residency, I did not re-apply for a position in my hospital. Rather I elected to stay silent and not mention whether I would like to stay or leave the next year, nor did they asked about my plans.

Shortly after the submission of my applications, the feared letters of rejection began to arrive one after the other, all of them regretting not having an opening. Time was passing, spring had come and still only negative responses were arriving.

However, by April, when my agony had crested, my most fortunate day had arrived. In midmorning while we were rounding I was overhead paged, which was then the quickest way to reach someone in the hospital. I called the operator who in turn connected me to the caller who was waiting on the line. Upon identifying me an imposing voice answered. "This is Dr. William Scott Jr., Chairman of the Department of Surgery at Vanderbilt University," he said. I did not know what to think when I heard the name. I certainly did not relate it to my search for residency, rather I thought the call concerned some patient in my hospital. Dr. Scott then went on to ask me whether I was still interested in a residency position. When I answered affirmatively, he said that he did not have such an opening but he could offer me a straight surgical internship, which in the long run would be advantageous to me. With great enthusiasm I told him that it would be a great privilege for me to take that position. His reply was that as of that moment the position was mine and that I soon would receive the letter of confirmation. Indeed a few days later I received the letter with some suggestions as to where and how to report on July first. I was overwhelmed by the offer and the way it happened. Over the past six months after the many repeated disappointing negative responses from the majority of the institutions to which I had applied almost all my hopes had vanished. To have this offer from a most admired institution be delivered by a personal phone call from the chairman of the department of surgery was more than I could have imagined.

In the next few days I informed the current hospital authorities that for the next academic year I would be moving elsewhere. They were probably expecting this news since I had not applied there for a residency position.

I took off the last few days of June to spend time with my relatives in Detroit before I moved south. They were happy for me because at last I had found the position that I was looking for although they preferred for me to have stayed in Detroit or in a close proximity.

VIII. THE MAKING OF A CARDIAC SURGEON

On July the first I took an early flight to Nashville. This was my first time that I had flown on an airplane. It was an awesome experience. The unlimited open space as we lifted into the blue sky appeared to me to represent the unlimited horizons that were possibly opening to me as I was moving to my new training program. I was extremely excited for this golden opportunity but I was equally concerned as to how I would fit into this prestigious institution and as to whether I would be able to meet their expectations.

According to the directions previously given to me, upon arrival at Vanderbilt hospital I went to the telephone operators. I was then told to wait at the entrance hall as they proceeded to call someone. Shortly afterwards three young men, the chief resident, Dr. Harold Collins and the two surgical assistants residents Drs. John Foster and John Sawyer arrived. We made our introductions and then I was asked to repeat my first name. I said "Panagiotis". They attempted to pronounce it correctly, but soon they gave up and said never mind, you are on call today so let us take you to the house staff quarters. The house was just a few steps away from the back door of the hospital. It was an old residential two-story building with a large porch in front facing the wide-open green university campus with its many majestic magnolia trees dispersed throughout it. The campus view from the porch was beautiful and soothing. I was led into a small room on the first floor with just enough space for a bunk bed and a small head table with a telephone and a lamp. What a coincidence, I thought! I left Greece from a similar size room. Did this similarity suggest that I would also live in this room during all my training and that these years might be as stimulating and creative as those that I spent in the student's house in Greece? As it happened, the answer turned out to be yes. I lived in that small room all the six years of my training which turned out to be equally as exciting and creative but thankfully less trying than those in Greece.

I changed into my house staff uniform and walked back into the hospital to become familiar with its various services. I visited the emergency rooms, the clinical laboratories, the surgical wards, the surgical suite, the cafeteria and the surgical research laboratories. All the areas except the research facilities were about the same as those that I had experienced the previous year. The surgical research laboratory was a unique and very impressive area to me. Its surgical theater was a large well-lit open area with ten operating room tables for large experimental animals. Next to it there was a modern clinical laboratory devoted only to all the tests required at the research facilities and there was modern housing for the experimental animals as well. A full time laboratory technician and two men, one, a surgical assistant and the other, a caretaker of the animals, staffed the area.

While I was going about my tour I suddenly heard the overhead operator paging Peter Symbas. Surprised I wondered who is this Peter Symbas? They could not be paging me I thought since my first name was not Peter and yet it could not possibly be somebody else since my last name was rare even in Greece. Therefore how could I encounter someone with my last name the first day in Nashville, especially at Vanderbilt hospital? I therefore decided to answer and solve the dilemma. Upon calling the operator I was told that Dr. Symbas was needed in the pediatric suite because a child, who the previous day had a craniotomy for a brain tumor was not doing well. Since I had previously been told that on that day I was on call for neurosurgery, it became obvious that the individual who was paged was I, even though my first name was different. After I took care of the child I went to inform the operators that my first name was not Peter. Their response was that Peter was the name, which was given to them by the chief surgical resident and that if I wanted to correct it I should speak to Dr. Collins. I was so grateful for being where I was that I did not mention the issue of my name again until three years later. Dr. Collins then told me that he had decided to arbitrarily name me Peter because my first name was so difficult to pronounce. Thusly, I was given the nickname Peter by which I am still called by the majority of colleagues and friends. My legal name remains Panagiotis. I was named Panagiotis because my great grand father's name was Panagiotis and perhaps because I was born on august fifteenth, the day that the Virgin Mary is celebrated in the Greek Orthodox Church.

The surgical training at Vanderbilt was then one year of straight surgical internship and five years of residency, the last year serving as chief resident. At the end of the sixth year the trainee was qualified for both the general and the thoracic surgical boards. It was a pyramidal program, meaning that in each one of the successive years someone was dropped off the slot, so that by the sixth year only three of the eight interns that had started the training program became chief residents. The rest either relocated to another program or dropped off to continue at another year. This system, as expected, put significant additional stress on the residents. Nobody knew until Christmas whether he would continue his training the next year or would be dropped either temporary or permanently from the slot. So the Christmas holidays were filled with great expectation for all of us not so much for the celebrations and the conventional presents but for the ultimate present that we were to receive from the director of the training program. We would find out whether we would continue our residency or not. I was fortunate enough to hear good news each Christmas at Vanderbilt which was that I would be able to continue my training.

Overall the entire training program was what I hoped for and more. There were many progressive both non-operative and operative patients' responsibilities and experiences, numerous teaching conferences, clinical research and above all, there was animal research opportunity. The research laboratory was available to all of us for voluntary participation whenever it was convenient as well as for a six-month compulsory rotation during the third year of our residency. During those times we could participate in ongoing projects or start our own project after the faculty had approved it.

The best of all teaching activities were the Saturday morning rounds with Dr. Scott, which started at eight in the morning and finished at ten o clock and beyond. They included the residents' complete presentation of each patient from the time of admission, review of the laboratories, including any radiographic tests, followed by questions and answers. Finally, Dr. Scott with his authoritative voice and his eloquent expressions would add many pertinent comments on each subject. The formal conduct of the rounds, the complete review of the patient's clinical course and Dr. Scott's most informative comments made those morning rounds an enjoyable and excellent learning experience.

This structure of the training program motivated every one of us to learn even more, to do our best work and even to compete with each other. As would be expected there was great competition among us but there was no under-cutting and no negative comments against each other. Instead there was support for each other. Perhaps this was the result of the unwritten and unspoken wishes and expectations of the faculty members. Everyone did their best to take care of their responsibilities and then let their destiny to be decided by the faculty.

The surgical faculty consisted of full time and part time or clinical faculty. The fulltime faculty had a limited number of private patients. In addition, however, they were overseeing the care of the indigent or ward patients and they also devoted much time to teaching and research. Their devotion to these activities and others made this department of surgery one of the most prominent in the country. In contrast, the clinical or part-time faculty was fully engaged in private practice with limited teaching activity.

Dr. Scott, the chairman of the department of surgery, was a handsome imposing man in his early forties. He was an eloquent speaker with a broad knowledge of the field of surgery. He was an excellent teacher and surgeon, devoted to his profession, a perfectionist, but also kind and supportive to his faculty and house staff. Although he was a disciplinarian he was never abusive or demeaning and he gracefully accepted challenges from his faculty and even from his residents. For example, on one Saturday morning during rounds I presented a patient that we had operated upon the previous night for traumatic injury to the popliteal artery. After I described the location of the popliteal vessels and nerve, he corrected me as to their relative positions. I replied that I was certain that my description was the correct one. All the residents were somewhat surprised with my stand.

Then following the verification that the location of the anatomical structures of the popliteal fossa was as I described it, Dr. Scott smiled and said, "good job." I was most pleasantly surprised and greatly relieved with his gracious response, which greatly amplified my respect and admiration for him.

The hospital patients were of different categories: private paying and indigent. The private physicians had the primary responsibility for the care of the private patients and a faculty member was assigned for the supervision of the care of the indigent patients. The private patients were housed in one-bed or two beds rooms whereas the indigent patients were in multi-bed wards. All the patients were segregated into wards for blacks and wards for whites. The house staff rotated through all the various services and took care of all the patients. The degree of the house staff's participation in the patients' care was dependent upon the seniority of the resident, upon the patient's status, private or ward, the individual resident's abilities and performance and upon the attending surgeon.

In addition, during our training years each one of us rotated at the Nashville Veteran's Administration Hospital and at the Nashville General Hospital. The Vanderbilt University residents provided the care to the patients at both institutions under the supervision of fulltime physicians employed by these hospitals. These physicians were also faculty members of Vanderbilt University.

My daily work as an intern was much harder than that of the previous year but much more structured, instructive and enjoyable. It consisted of early morning rounding by myself to see each of the patients assigned to our service, changing dressings, drawing blood for the tests to be done and writing orders and progress notes. Then on the way to the cafeteria for breakfast I would unload all the blood samples, which filled all the pockets of my uniform, dropped the x-ray requisitions off and by seven o'clock I was in the operating theater. There I shaved, positioned, scrubbed, and draped the patient and assisted the operating surgeon. This went on until the day's operating schedule was over which could be at mid or late afternoon or into the night. After the schedule was over I worked up the new patients and finished any loose ends with the care of the old patients before or after supper and then rounded with the senior or chief resident. The call schedule was every other night and every other weekend, but I did not sign out until all my work was finished which was usually late at night. All my limited free time I devoted to reviewing the subjects of the cases that I was taking care of and the operative procedures that I was to participate in the next day. This form of studying provided me a review of the diseases that I was treating, prepared me for the expected quizzing by the senior resident or attending and afforded me a progressive review of the surgical textbooks and literature. As a result, during that year I left the hospital premises only on an occasional weekend and during my two-week vacation with my relatives in Detroit.

My first and second year of residency passed almost in a similar manner except that on Saturdays or in the evenings whenever I could, I would go to the surgical research laboratory where the first work on extracorporeal circulation and potassium induced cardiac arrest was conducted by residents and faculty. Sustaining life without the heart functioning, and manipulating the heart in various ways, stopping and starting it at will, was a mesmerizing experience. Although I had previously considered specializing in Neurosurgery, this experience and the frequent undesirable outcomes following surgical intervention upon the central nervous system changed my plans from devoting my efforts to Neurosurgery, to the new frontier of cardiac surgery. It seemed that the entire research laboratory was full of activity, excitement and creativity, as if everyone was trying to add a brick or two to the new skyscraper of cardiac surgery that had began to be built. This strong wind of excitement pushed me into the path of trying to conceive my own research project. As a result, a fraction of my limited available time for sleep I spent searching for an idea. At the end of my second year residency the answer to my search came to me when I was retracting the enlarged non-compliant cirrhotic liver during the performance of the anastomosis between the vena cava and portal vein. During the procedure and during the night hours I kept thinking that there must be a less tasking way for the surgeon and especially for the assistant to perform the connection between these two vessels. Then graft interposition in the peripheral arterial system was a common practice. As a result I reasoned that by interposing a graft between the portal vein and inferior vena cava, the portal cava shunt could be done with less efforts and trauma to the patient and to the surgical team. Although the prevailing view then was that interposition of a graft into the venous system would not work due to low pressure and low velocity of flow, I thought that for the setting that I was considering it might work because of the different pressures between the two venous systems, high in the portal vein and low in the inferior vena cava.

Although at the time of the conception of the project I was very excited, soon my excitement was toned down by the thought that, since my concept was so simple, most likely it had already been tested. I therefore could not wait to find time to search the literature. The following weekend I spent it in the library. I was greatly surprised and relieved when I determine that my concept had not been investigated. I then presented my idea to one of the clinical faculty Dr. Andrew Dale, who in his practice had predominantly dealt with vascular and particularly with venous problems. I was greatly disappointed when he immediately dismissed my idea as a non-workable concept. After this set back, I met with the then, young faculty member, Dr. John Foster, hoping to get his approval for my project. Thankfully, he did not disappoint me. He not only felt strongly that the concept was sound and deserved an investigation but he was very excited about it.

Before my regular assignment in the surgical research laboratory, I began my project using the great technical skills and assistance of a wonderful man, the lab assistant, Mr. Andrew. Then during my six months required rotation in the lab, we first demonstrated that venous graft interposition and then prosthetic graft interposition between the portal vein and vena cava remained patented. A few months later we presented our results at the annual meeting of the Society of University Surgeons. This experience confirmed to me that listening to the ideas of our seniors in medicine is important, but that their ideas should not to be taken as dogma particularly if they had not been critically tested.

Later on Dr. Foster performed a portal caval shunt, with graft interposition, in a young cirrhotic patient with bleeding esophageal varices. Subsequently, several investigators embraced this procedure especially Dr. Drepanas who greatly popularized it to the point that it was temporary labeled "Drepanas procedure."

This mislabel, however, was corrected by our previous chairman of the department of Surgery at Emory, Dr. Dean Warren, who as I was told by him, at an annual meeting of vascular surgery set the record straight, indicating that the procedure was first investigated by me and that it was later clinically performed by Dr. Foster. So much for the correctness of some of the eponyms.

As I mentioned earlier, I came to my new country with the intention of permanently establishing myself in the United States. As a result early on I started investigating the possibility of obtaining a license to practice here. Out of the many states that I explored, only Michigan indicated that I could take the two parts of the state board, after I appeared for some form of oral examination that the state then required for foreign graduates. I was informed that the examination was scheduled to be given at Wayne State University and so I traveled there. Upon entering the designated exam room I was met by few men sitting around a large table. Apparently they were faculty members of the medical school. I was directed to sit on one of the chairs at the head of the table.

The scene looked to me like the Last Supper that Jesus had experienced. Immediately I began to wonder would that be my last supper too or the beginning of the fulfillment of many dreams to come. Each of the men asked me straightforward medical questions from their respected fields. I managed to answer all of them until the last one, which was related to psychiatry. Not knowing the answer and having felt good about the examination up to that time, I indicated that I did not know the answer, and parenthetically added that I did not intend to practice psychiatry. All the other examiners, except the one who asked the question, laughed. Nevertheless, I passed. Shortly afterwards, I was notified that I could take part one of the State Board, which I did and before the end of my third year of residency I took part two and obtained my license in the state of Michigan.

During my fourth year of residency special national written examinations for the qualification of foreign graduates was established. During that year they were scheduled to be given at Vanderbilt hospital in Nashville for the candidates who resided in the southeastern states. Although I did not need to take these examinations since I was already licensed to practice medicine in Michigan State, because of the convenience of taking them at my home institution, I enrolled and passed them. Having passed the State Board of Michigan and also this board, I was given the right to apply for practice in any state that I chose.

Since the end of the Greek civil war in 1949 both my brother John and I were hopelessly trying to determine the fate of our parents and of the rest of our family, searching through various agencies and especially through the international Red Cross. We did not know whether they were living or dead or where they were taken. First we found that our older brother Naum along with his family were initially taken to Romania and later were moved to Skopie, a Yugoslavian city close to the northern Greek border. Subsequently, my two nieces, the daughters of my oldest sister Vasiliki, who were separated and one of them was taken to Czechoslovakia and the other to Yugoslavia, both were permitted to go join their father, who was living in Australia. Finally in 1956 we were informed by the Red Cross that our parents were still living and they were with my oldest sister Vasiliki in Poland (Figure 11). Later on my sister was permitted to go to Australia and join her husband and daughters, and my parents were allowed to return to Greece. Afterwards my other sister Anna, with her husband who had been taken to Russia were also permitted to return to Greece and they subsequently immigrated to America.

**Figure 11
Photo of my parents and my sister Vasiliki in
Poland.**

On the way home my parents stopped in Yugoslavia to see my brother Naum and his family after their long and arduous separation. During the visit my brother Naum begged my parents to stay with him and his family instead of going to Greece where no family member still lived. Then my father told my brother Naum that although he would love to be with him and his family, but even though no one from our family was still in Greece and all of our tangible property was destroyed, his motherland was still there and that he would return to his native country where he belonged, and that there he would take his last breath, as indeed he later did.

The clinical rotations during the last half of my third year and fourth year of residency passed with a similar pace of work as that of the previous years, but with greater clinical and especially surgical participation and also more autonomy and greater pleasure and satisfaction from my constant professional growth.

As I have mentioned earlier all my previous Christmases at Vanderbilt were full of anxiety, followed by great relief and satisfaction, but the Christmas of the fourth year of my residency was the most anxious one of all. Again to my pleasant surprise I was chosen to move up in my training, which in addition to the privilege of becoming chief resident I was afforded the title of instructor and greater salary.

Our salary during the internship year was only twenty-five dollars per month. During the four years of residency it was seventy-five dollars per month and during the chief residency it was increased to five hundred dollars per month. In addition every year we were provided with a room free of charge and free meals at the hospital cafeteria. Since all my life then revolved around my work, this compensation was more than enough for me up to my chief residency. So with five hundred dollars monthly salary during my chief residency I considered myself rich, since up to that time I had never received such a sizeable salary.

After I was awarded the chief residency I decided to take my first trip back to my Greek homeland before I started my chief residency. I wrote to my cousin Argyri Paparyriou to purchase an automobile for me, a new Volkswagen Beetle, and on April I flew to Paris. After an emotional and enjoyable visit with Argyri and his family he gave me a brief demonstration on how to drive my new car, which had stick shift that I never practiced before. There I encountered a mutual friend who asked me if he could accompany me to Greece. I wanted a companion and so we left together. Trying to get out of Paris in the afternoon when the traffic was over congested and in the midst of the chaotic Parisian driving was a tasking experience, if not a suicidal one.

We started our trip with a traveling map of Europe but no plans as to where we would stop and where we would sleep. We traversed France, Switzerland, Northern Italy and Yugoslavia with stops wherever we encountered something of interest. At night we lodged in houses, which offered sleeping facilities for

THE VOYAGE OF A SHEPHERD BOY

a minimal price with full trust to our hosts, which each time proved to be justifiable. Moving from country to country after a relatively small distance of travel, and encountering different customs, language, food and different architecture, was a wonderful experience.

Our last stop was in Skopie Yugoslavia to see my brother Naum and his family. I was most happy and anxious to visit with him after almost fourteen years of separation but I also had considerable misgivings about seeing some of my villagers, including my primary school classmate Dimitri Zisiadi, who were then residing there. Perhaps some of them may have been instrumental for my exile to Slimista, during the tragic civil war years

On the one hand I somewhat wanted to meet them again after so many tragic events that had intervened since our last encounter. On the other hand I dreaded the prospect that I might have to face the same resentment and even animosity that some of them had shown me during the wars. Surprisingly I was received with some warmth and admiration and no visible resentment.

It was most gratifying to me to see that my brother Naum, although unhappy for being in Yugoslavia was doing reasonably well. In addition, despite his frugal lifestyle his children were being educated and were excelling. Sad but comforted, after a couple of days I left for Greece. Crossing the border into Greece was indeed rejuvenating. There were wild flowers everywhere, the fields were meticulously cultivated, the plants were in full growth and all the traces of the war were eliminated except for the bunkers, which lay in ruins, covered with abundant bushes, as if they were trying to conceal those chilly reminders of our tragic civil war. After several hours drive, we arrived in Kastoria where my parents were residing after their return from Poland. Seeing and touching them again after fourteen years of separation and with no knowledge as to whether they were alive was an indescribably wonderful feeling. Although they had aged, my father was now in his late seventies and considerably worn out, my parents were very happy and thankful for having returned home and especially for discovering that all their children and grandchildren not only had survived those treacherous years but they were thriving, and were excelling (Figure 12). Despite my parents' obvious happiness and satisfaction with their life, I thought it might be better for them to come to live in America. One day while my father and I were sitting in the shade of the platani and next to the calm reflective water of the lake, I expressed my idea to him. He replied, "I love America because I lived and worked there for several years. It is a wonderful country and full of opportunities, but not for me at my age. I took those opportunities when it was my turn but now I belong here." He enjoyed the remaining six years of his life periodically visiting his beloved farm and his village. He would take a walk everyday alone or with his friends around the peninsula and the beautiful lake of Kastoria. He was certainly thankful for what life overall had offered to him. He took his last breath in his own free, peaceful country and his bones are resting in the most prominent and picturesque site of his farm.

During my two weeks stay in Greece I nostalgically traced all the previous steps of my life there. I visited our farm area, our village, my aunt Katerina and her family, my high school, my university, the students' house, and my friends, my two great officers, Mr. Tsekouras and Dr. Vellios and even Cape Sounion. There standing at the Temple of Posidon I scanned for a while the infamous island of Makronisos. All these visits evoked sadness and pleasure, gratification and gratitude but mercifully no remorse or anger.

The shipment of my car to the states was arranged through La Havre, France. As a result a few days before I was expected to be at my job, with Vangelli Arvanitis, an old friend from my village and then residing in Canada, we left Kastoria for France.

THE VOYAGE OF A SHEPHERD BOY

Figure 12
Photo with my partents, my sister Anna, her two daughters, and others in our farm area during my first trip to Greece. Me between my father and mother.

Leaving my parents once more and not knowing whether we would see each other again was heartbreaking for all of us. My father's aged, stoic, and strong face gave in to the deeply hidden sadness clouding his eyes, and my mother could not stop her tears. I drove off with the sense that I was abandoning them. I was very saddened, yet satisfied, knowing that they were spending the rest of their lives happy and where they wanted to be.

We left the Greek soil from the northwestern coast on a ferryboat to Brindizi, a port on the southwestern coast of Italy. It was early afternoon on a clear day, when the boat sailed in the Ionian Sea. Sitting on its deck I could see as far as the peaks of Mountain Olympus. As we moved westward, I once more waved a farewell to the sun-bathed, gray green mainland decorated with clusters of white-walled and red roofed houses. They were dispersed into the slopes of the mountains, from the bosom of the dark blue sea into the open light blue sky.

We were now again in my automobile which had been ferried across with the two of us to Brindizi. Driving, we crossed from east to west, the Italian peninsula. The night was clear, moonless, and dark. We ascended the mountains, driving on a lonely, narrow, curvy, two-way road. Half way down of our descent from the mountain in the early hours of the morning we began to see sporadically flickering lights on the road. Each of the lights was a kerosene lamp hanging on the end of many buggies, which were carrying produce to the city. I cautiously passed them one after the other without reducing my speed since the traffic was going exclusively along our, direction. Around five o'clock in the morning we had descended from the mountains and now we were traveling on a wider but straight, flat road with gigantic plane trees lined up on both its sides. They were covering the road with their branches forming a large green tunnel. As we continued passing the dimly lit buggies, I suddenly faced a similar flickering light but this one was not hanging from a buggy but from the wing of an airplane. The aircraft was apparently disabled and several Italians were hauling it in the middle of the road in the opposite direction of traffic, and of course, straight in our way. Because of the darkness I was only about thirty feet away when I noticed the small airplane. Pressing my brakes I managed to stop the car, but I was so close that the edge of its wing almost touched the windshield of my car. It was a most frightening and bizarre experience, fortunately resulting in no injuries and only in a small scratch of the driver's side door. When angrily we questioned the men as to why they did not display a more conspicuous signal during this dangerous undertaking, dismissively, they said that they were not expecting a car at that weird hour.

After narrowly escaping decapitation, we traveled to Neapolis, Rome, Pisa, Milan, Venice, and Genoa. Then after traveling along the Mediterranean coast of Italy and France we went to Monaco, Marseilles, Lyon and finally to Paris. We were enchanted while visiting Rome with all its antiquates, Pisa with its leaning tower and its old learning institutions, Venice with its enchanting canals and all its beautiful cathedrals and squares and Monaco with its glittering casinos and shops. Above all we felt overwhelmingly charmed traveling along the pristine Mediterranean coast of Italy and France with its extensive fields of blossoming flowers on one side, and the blue water of the sea on the other side.

Shortly after the return from my trip I began my final year of residency with great joy and hidden pride. The workload continued as it had in previous years but the responsibilities increased, since the chief resident was responsible for overseeing the care of all general and cardiothoracic surgical patients. Although occasionally agonizing and painful, the opportunity, to oversee the care of all patients, to operate independently, to choose the cases on which to operate and to be more involved in teaching, made the year most rewarding and enjoyable.

During that year I felt confident enough to perform independently most any general or cardio thoracic surgical procedure except for those which required the use of extracorporeal circulation. The latter were performed exclusively by the faculty, Dr. Scott, but more commonly by Dr. Collins. This was because open-heart surgery was then in its infancy. Every step from the surgical procedures, to the extracorporeal circulation unit itself, and to the management of its adverse effects upon the patient was in an embryonic stage. As a result, each operative procedure was a big project in itself and the outcome unfortunately some times undesirable. During each operation the operating room was overcrowded with large primitive recording equipment, the extracorporeal unit and numerous personnel. They included the surgeon and his two assistants, the anesthesiologist and his assistant, the perfusionist, the recorder who was responsible for the monitoring equipment, the two scrub nurses and also two other circulating nurses.

Everyone was somewhat tense and focused on his or her task. The operating surgeon, with hidden tension, displayed calmness and confidence trying to inspire similar feelings to his team. The operating theater buzzed from activities and verbal exchanges until the point of commencement of the extracoporeal circulation and of the intracardiac procedure. At this point the only conversation was that between the surgeon and his assistants, his perfusionist, the anesthesiologist and the recorder. Everyone else would occasionally whisper or stand silent, anxiously waiting the moment when the patient was separated from the extracorporeal circulation and the heart began its normal function. Then a great sense of relief was displayed by everyone in the room, except for the physicians, whose relief was guarded. The physicians then enjoyed the outcome of the first face of the patient's care but we feared the next several hours when the adverse effects of the operation and especially those of the extracorporeal circulation, were manifested. Spending the whole postoperative night at the patient's bedside trying to treat the respiratory, metabolic, hematologic, and hemodynamic abnormalities after surgery was like fighting an enemy with an unknown and unpredictable destructive force with insufficient or totally unavailable means. This led to triumph, satisfaction, and pure joy when the battle was won and the patient's health and heart were restored. Sometimes it led to helplessness, desperation, and bitterness when the battled was lost.

Because the open-heart surgical field was new and rapidly expanding and because relatively few such procedures were performed by the midst of my chief residency year I did not feel ready to independently care for patients requiring open-heart surgery. As a result, I decided to take an additional year of training devoting it exclusively to cardiac surgery. Dr. Scott informed me that there were four centers, which offered such opportunities. With his recommendation I chose and I was accepted into Dr. Rollin Hanlon's Cardiac Surgical fellowship program at Saint Louis University.

As my chief residency was approaching its end, I nostalgically began to look back over the last six years. The beautiful city of Nashville with its pristine large wooded Warner Park, and the modern replica of the Parthenon next door to Vanderbilt, the hospitable personnel of the hospital, my friendly and helpful colleagues and the kind, caring, supportive faculty dedicated to the resident's training made my tenure at Vanderbilt most enjoyable, rewarding, and instructive. In addition Dr. Scott's dedication to teaching and patient care, his technical perfection and his caring for everyone's well being, especially for his residents, became the beacon that I have tried to follow (Figure 13).

**Surgical Staff
Vanderbilt University Hospital – Thayer Veterans
Administration Hospital
1961-1962**

1st row: Gobbel, Foster, Zukoski, McSwain, Stephenson, Scott, Meachan, Sawyers, Fleming, Shoulders, Stoney, Adkins, Waltzer
2nd row: Rhea, Campbell, Turman, Hays, Carlisle, Guest, Nelson, Richie, Vasko, Wheeler, Tyler
Not present: Alford, Bomar, Bond, Callaway, Collins, Davis, Fischer, Goodman, Harlowe, Hillman, Hunt, Jacob, Jacobs, Jolly, Jones, J., Jones, O., Kaplan, Lee, Luther, McConnell, McCullough, O'Neill, Sachatello, Sessions, Shelly, Smith, Snyder, Trapp, Turner, Williams, Woodhead, Youmans.

**Figure 13
Group photo at the end of my chief residency at Vanderbilt**

IX. POLISHING THE CARDIAC SURGEON

On July third, with a few belongings, loaded in my Volkswagen beetle, I left Nashville with overwhelming gratitude to Dr. Scott and to everybody that I had worked with and with the sense that I was leaving my second hometown.

July fourth was a typical hot and muggy summer, St. Louis day. I woke up early in the morning anxious to familiarize myself with my new environment. I drove to De Lodge hospital, which was an old gothic style, impressive building. I walked to the first floor where the offices of the department of surgery were located but due to the holiday no one was around. Then I went to Cardinal Gleenon Children's hospital, which was a modern, relatively new structure located on the other side of the block. De Lodge was an adult and Cardinal Gleenon was a pediatric hospital. Both of them were operated by Jesuits and the Sister's of Mercy. At the Children's hospital I met the chief surgical resident who gave me a grand tour of both hospitals. The composition of patients at both of them was like that at Vanderbilt, both private pay and indigent patients.

On July the fifth, early in the morning I met Dr. Hanlon, a distinguished, tall, slim, pleasant, creative, and extremely knowledgeable man. Early in his career he along with Dr. Alfred Blalock developed the closed atrial septectomy procedure for the treatment of the transposition of the great vessels. His knowledge of the world was rivaled only by his knowledge of medicine. It was intimidating for me to engage with him even in the topics of classic Greece even though I was educated in Greece. His conduct in every aspect was exemplary. It was indeed inspiring to work with him. He welcomed me, introduced me to his secretary and asked her to help me with whatever I needed.

The department of General and Cardiothoracic surgery then had three fulltime faculty members, Dr. Hanlon, who was the chairman and Drs. Willman and Cooper as well as several part-time, faculty members. Their clinical and teaching work was similar to that of the faculty at Vanderbilt except for Dr. Cooper who devoted almost all his efforts to research and teaching. The volume of open-heart procedures was greater than that at Vanderbilt, and the greater portion of them was for congenital lesions. However, after October, when the first report appeared on the availability of satisfactory prosthetic heart valves and their first clinical applications, the volume of valve replacement cases for acquired lesions increased significantly.

Most of the patients had advanced stages of cardiac disease, especially those with acquired lesions, who had severely compromised cardiac function. As a result, not infrequently, their intraoperative and postoperative course was difficult and complicated, and as would be expected sometime, less than ideal. The intraoperative complications such as the inability occasionally of the heart to resume its workload, or the persistent bleeding from diffuse oozing frequently kept us in the operating room for long exhausting hours. Then after, postoperatively frequently the patients had bleeding and low cardiac output which required us to spend many night hours at the patients bedside trying to remedy these and many other adversities. Dr. Hanlon's dedication to his patients was an inspiration to me. He never indicated any sign of desperation or fatigue; rather he faced all adversities with calm, determination and confidence. He stayed with his patients late into the night or into the early morning hours, even when he could not personally offer them anything more than we could.

My responsibility during that year was to supervise the care of cardiac patients and to participate in all their surgical procedures. In addition, one day of the week I participated in the ongoing investigation by Dr. Willman on experimental cardiac transplantation and carried on my own research project on cardiac lymphatics and the effects upon the heart following their permanent interruption. In addition, in the autumn of that year, I took the first part of the general surgical boards. In February of the next year I passed their second part and by May I had passed both the general surgical and the cardiothoracic boards. All the above activities during my fellowship year made its passing enjoyable and unnoticeable.

Although, as I had mentioned earlier, I came to this country with the full intention to permanently stay here, as my training period was approaching its end, I began to entertain the possibility of returning to Greece. My persistent nostalgia for my native country, the social aspect of life there and the desire to contribute to the establishment of the open-heart surgery unit at my alma mater, were the motivating forces for considering returning to my country.

These forces were enhanced by the enticing suggestions of a couple of chairmen of the departments of surgery in Greece whom I had met at international meetings. They appeared to be fully aware of my career and they asked me to consider the possibility of joining their department.

During that time, Dr. Hanlon asked me what I was planning for the following year. I told him then that I loved the professional life here but I was still missing the other aspects of the life in Greece. I also added that it would be very fulfilling for me if I could contribute to the development of cardiac surgery there. His reply was that he understood my feelings and commended me for my desires.

Until that point in my career I had focused only on my training. I was totally naive as to how to seek employment, how to negotiate a permanent position and worst of all, I was too bashful to ask anyone for guidance. Therefore, even though I was uneasy about the offer, and without reasonable security that I would find what I wanted, I decided to go back to Greece to determine whether any of these suggestions were suitable for me. Unfortunately it did not take too long after my arrival there to find out that what was available was anything but what I wanted. I was offered to be one of the many assistants, albeit paid, who was to follow the chairman around without substantial identity for an undefined period of time. Certainly that was not what I was seeking.

After a prolonged vacation in Greece, I returned to St. Louis somewhat disappointed. On my first day back at the university, quite embarrassed because of my unsuccessful attempt to secure a job in Greece, I met Dr. Hanlon. After I narrated my visit in Greece, he kindly indicated that he was sorry for that, and added that he had filled the vacancy in his department, but I could stay with him until I could find a suitable job.

Later on at the annual meeting of the Society of Thoracic Surgery I briefly met Dr. Allen Macris and his wife, a pleasant Greek couple from Atlanta. Shortly after my return to St. Louis I received a telephone call from Allen asking me if I would consider coming to Atlanta to work with him.

During previous years whenever I was asked where I would prefer to live, Atlanta was one of the places that I entertained. Since Atlanta was one of my choices for permanent residency and I still had no permanent job, even though I always planned to pursue an academic career, the offer that I was given was an acceptable one at least as a first step.

After I decided to take the offer in Atlanta I informed Dr. Hanlon that, by necessity, I would be moving there and that I would still continue to seek an opportunity for an academic career. I left St. Louis with no enthusiasm about where I was going and most importantly what I would be doing.

Driving south I stopped in Nashville to see my mentor Dr. Scott. During dinner at his house I narrated what had transpired the previous year and a half, what I would be doing in the immediate future and what I wanted to do for the rest of my professional life. He wished me well and comforted me by stressing that eventually the type of permanent job that I was looking for would be found. This statement somewhat lifted my spirits and I left Nashville with guarded optimism about my future.

X. ACADEMIC LIFE

My work in Atlanta was anticlimactic after that of my last two years. It was limited to the general thoracic surgical field; bronchoscopies, pulmonary resections, and very limited esophageal surgery, mainly hiatal heniorrhaphy. Fortunately this form of work did not last long. About three months after my arrival in Atlanta I received a telephone call from Dr. Osler Abbott the chief of the Cardiothoracic Surgical section at Emory University. He informed me that he was planning to add a new faculty member in his section and that Dr. Scott and Dr. Hanlon had suggested that he contact me. He also asked me whether I would be interested in such a job. I replied that I always wanted to pursue an academic career and we agreed to meet and discuss the issue.

Dr. Abbott was rather heavyset, over-confident, flamboyant, verbose, but a very articulate man. At our first meeting at his office at the Emory Clinic he greeted me warmly, asked me a few questions and went on to tell me that he wanted someone to develop and head the Cardiothoracic Surgical Program at Grady Hospital. He then took me to the office of the Chairman of the Department of Surgery where I met Dr. J.D. Martin. With great formality and perhaps restrained enthusiasm, Dr. Martin asked me several questions concerning my background and about my experiences at Vanderbilt and St. Louis University and then I returned to Dr. Abbott's office somewhat discouraged. However, to my surprise, Dr. Abbott offered me the job with an appointment as an instructor of the department of surgery, and asked me to let him know about my decision in about a week. I left the Emory campus with mixed emotions. I was happy because of the opportunity to finally begin the academic career that I had been dreaming of and in one of the cities of my choice, but intimidated and fearful of the responsibilities that I was to assume. During the next couple of days I called my mentor Dr. Scott and informed him about the offer and asked for his advice. He encouraged me to accept the job and assured me that I would do well. With Dr. Scott's encouragement and my great desire to start my academic life, I called Dr. Abbot and told him that I would be honored to join his department. He warmly welcomed my decision and referred me to his secretary for all the administrative steps that I needed to take for my appointment.

Until then the only thing that I knew of Grady Hospital was the scientific contributions, which had been reported from it, such as the management of penetrating cardiac wounds by Dr. Elkin and the first cardiac catheterization performed in this country by Drs. Weens and Stead.

On my first visit to Grady I found its imposing gigantic gray structure very intimidating. The copy of the statue of Hygieia in an alcove on one side of its main entrance and that of Hippocrates on the other side were inspiring and reminded me of my ancestral obligations towards the patients that would be coming there to receive healthcare. The hospital was much larger than any of those where I had previously worked and had a bed capacity of about nine hundred from the fourth to the twelfth floors. Each floor had four wards with multiple beds in each of them, and sliding cloth curtains surrounded each bed to be used when privacy was needed. In addition, there were two beds rooms for sicker patients. Unfortunately, for the first two years after my appointment with Emory, the patients were segregated into black and white wards. All of them were indigent and were cared for by the housestaff and faculty of the Emory University School of Medicine.

THE VOYAGE OF A SHEPHERD BOY

The major portion of the clinical teaching in the School of Medicine as well as the clinical research activities were then carried out at the Grady campus. All the chairmen of the clinical departments had offices on the Grady campus, Dr. J. Willis Hurst, the Chairman of the Department of Medicine, Dr. J.D. Martin, the Chairman of the Department of Surgery, Dr. G.Blumberg, the Chairman of the Department of Pediatrics, Dr. J. D.Thompson, the Chairman of the Department of Obstetrics and Gynecology, and Dr. H. Weems, the Chairman of Radiology. In addition, Dr. Robert Schlant and Dr. Nanette Wenger and others from the Division of Cardiology, Dr. Katherine Edwards and Dr. Dorothy Brinsfield from the Division of Pediatric Cardiology, and Dr. H. Harlan Stone, Dr. J. Richard, A. Emerson, and Dr. Ira Ferguson from the Department of Surgery all had offices on the Grady campus. The hospital was vibrating with excellent patient care, teaching and research activities. There was constant interaction between members of the faculty on the floors, in the lounges, and in the cafeteria with the constant generation of new ideas. It was an inspiring, stimulating, and creative academic environment and remained so for many years afterwards.

My office was located on the third floor of the hospital in the D section and remained there throughout my 43 years of tenure at Emory. The operating rooms, the recovery room and later the Surgical Intensive Care Unit were also located on the third floor. This location, because of its proximity to all the above areas and especially to the recovery room and the Intensive Care Unit, facilitated my prompt response to any of the emergencies that our patients manifested in those areas, which were then quite frequent, and life-threatening.

My first secretary was Mrs. Gerry Brown, a very pleasant, kind and helpful woman. Her dedication, loyalty, and work ethic were exemplary. She began working for me one week after I started and continued for over 20 years until she retired. She made my work easier and productive. In addition to the routine office work, she kept records of all patients who we treated and she typed and re-typed multiple versions of our articles and books until they were finalized. It was indeed a great privilege and pleasure to work with such a nice individual during those demanding and creative years.

I began working for Emory on July 1, 1964. My assignment was to head the Cardiothoracic Surgical Service at Grady Memorial Hospital and care for all of the cardiothoracic patients. In addition, I had to participate in the teaching of the senior medical school class and of our residents, to carry on administrative duties for both institutions, Emory and Grady and also to carry on my research.

1. TEACHING THE STUDENTS

The student's curriculum then required that all the pertinent topics of cardiothoracic surgery be taught to the senior medical school class. At that time almost the entire senior medical class lectures were held at the Grady campus. The assignment for the Cardiothoracic Surgical lectures was equally divided between the faculty members of our section including Drs. O. Abbott, W. Logan, C.R. Hatcher and myself. After Dr. Abbott retired and Dr. Logan left, the teaching responsibilities were shared equally initially between Dr. C.R. Hatcher, Dr. K. Mansour and myself, later on between the three of us and Dr. E. Jones, Dr. J. Craver, Dr. J. Miller and Dr. Williams. Unfortunately, in addition to my assigned time for lecturing, I would frequently be called either the previous night or more commonly hours or minutes before the lecture to substitute for someone else since I was the only one stationed on the Grady campus. The usual reason was that whoever was supposed to lecture was tied up in the operating room at Emory or somewhere else. This issue sometimes aggravated me, particularly when the same person did it repeatedly. Before each lecture I would always attempt to review the topic and prepare visual material, highlighting the pertinent points of the lecture that I wanted the students to take with them after leaving the lecture hall.

Walking in front of the class as a junior faculty member, particularly during the first months and years of my tenure, was a daunting experience. The palms of my hands would sweat, my pulse would race and I wondered whether I would meet the expectations of the eager students. Would their precious time, either at seven o'clock in the morning or in the mid-afternoon, be productive or wasted? This wondering became more intense when I noticed that someone during the lecture was sleeping, a not uncommon occurrence. Did he fall asleep because he had been on call the previous night, because the lecture room was stuffy and the lights were dimmed, or because my lecture was boring, uninformative or tiring? I never heard that the latter was the reason for some of the student's mental absence, but it was comforting to me to see that almost always all the students were present during my lectures and I usually had several of them come to me after the lecture for more information or questions.

Although, as I said previously my earlier lecturing was both daunting and time-consuming, it was always equally exciting then and afterwards. Having so many pairs of eyes, some of them sharp and bright, and other dazzling, all trying to get something from the lecture, which would be of value to them in the future, was a wonderful and inspiring experience. My student teaching tenure lasted about thirty years, until the site of the lectures moved from the Grady to the Emory campus.

2. TEACHING THE RESIDENTS

Teaching the Cardiothoracic surgical residents was more difficult and sometimes agonizing. The aim was to equip them with factual knowledge, to help them master the art of Cardiothoracic Surgery and to acquire judgment and technical skills. The first aim, in such a bright and extremely motivated group of men, was easy to accomplish with the various teaching exercises, conferences, and rounds, and even during informal interaction during rest or while waiting for an operation to start. To attain the second aim was more difficult and sometimes agonizing; as I am sure it is for everyone involved in the training of residents.

In order to acquire judgment and skills it is essential for the residents to perform the entire operative procedures several times. It is well-established that observing and assisting alone cannot provide the needed experience, and especially technical proficiency. It requires "hands on experience" performing operative procedures many times. It is also well-established that when a patient needed care, he or she deserved to receive the best available one by the defined surgeon. Balancing these two established facts was the difficult part of my job.

Each resident rotating in our service had been fully trained in General Surgery and also had initially one and later on two years of Cardiothoracic surgical experience, but he or she was still in the ascending limb of the curve for mastering Cardiac surgical procedures. Also, the first several years of my tenure were the strategic years of the development of Cardiac surgery. Cardiopulmonary bypass machines were still primitive and our knowledge of pathological, physiological and neurohumoral changes that occurred during open heart procedures and their possible effects upon patients were still in an embryonic stage, as was our knowledge and ability to manage those issues. Doing the operation flawlessly and in as short a time as possible on cardiopulmonary bypass time were the surest ways to have the best outcome. The dilemma, though, was how to do that and yet to give to both parties what they rightfully expected i.e., the residents the chance to master all the operative procedures and the patient to get the best possible care. Keeping the patients' best interests first, my personal interest last and the residents' interest in between made it possible to mitigate the agonizing moments during the residents' training.

In the early years of my career when the risk of open-heart surgery was high, I alone had to perform the critical portion of all the major operations in order to secure the best possible results even though I would sense the unspoken disappointment of some of my residents for not doing it themselves. Later on, when open cardiac surgery was better developed, its side effects upon patients were better understood and their management became possible and especially when effective means of myocardial preservation during surgery became available, the resident performed all the operative procedures. Closely guiding the resident through all the entire procedure and providing good exposure of the operative field coupled with the personal talent of each trainee allowed me to meet the objectives of both the patients and the residents.

Seeing the patient's recovery from their illness and the resident's exponential mastering of the art of cardiac surgery was a humbling and most rewarding experience. This experience was made possible by the resident's hard work, dedication and inner talent, which sometimes would not manifest until we were ready to see it and devote the required time to nurture it. The latter point is illustrated with the following incident. During the second year of Dr. C.B.'s training, he was thought to be "struggling" by some of our faculty members and the wisdom of continuing his training with us was questioned. At one of the residents' progress review meetings in our section some of my colleagues suggested that he should be dismissed from our program. Although he had worked with me for a short time, I did not feel that he was, as some perceived him, "unsalvageable". Also, I could not rationalize how he had been kept working with us for two years and then we suddenly decided that he was "unsuitable" to be a cardiac surgeon. Therefore, I disagreed with the proposal for his dismissal. Then, one of the colleagues suggested that since I disagreed with the proposal, this resident should be sent for a long rotation with me at Grady, which was unanimously accepted. This young man, with no significantly greater nurturing from me than that which I provided to the other residents who rotated before and afterwards in our service did very well during his rotation with me and provided very good care to our patients. Similarly, not only did he continue to provide excellent care to his patients after he finished his training, also he rescued a failing cardiothoracic surgical program as well.

One of the greatest joys and rewards of my professional career was the opportunity to interact, work and see our trainees become talented cardiac surgeons and to have the privilege to be a small part of their professional life.

3. RESEARCH

Soon after I began my tenure at Emory, I initiated my research activities. My work was performed in a limited space on the third floor of the old medical library building on the Emory campus. A year or so later the Woodruff extension research building at the Grady campus was renovated, and almost $^2/_3$ of its basement area was allocated to the Department of Surgery for research. We had one large operating room area there with 5 tables for surgery on large experimental animals. In addition, there were 2 other rooms with a single similar operating table, a biochemical laboratory, and a utility room. The area was completely equipped using grant money from the National Institutes of Health and the periodic infusion of equipment from other research or clinical areas, which were replaced by new ones. It was staffed by two lab technicians, as well, and almost any research project could be performed there.

It was a busy area, where three surgical faculty members carried on their research, Dr. Converse Pierce was doing fulltime research, and Dr. H. Harlan Stone and I did part-time research joined by one surgical resident. Dr. Pierce was the director of the laboratory for two years, and, after he moved, the directorship was given to me. I continued directing it for almost thirty years when all the surgical research activities moved away from the Grady campus.

During those years we carried out numerous investigations, including but not limited to the following: the mode of drainage of the cardiac lymph after ligation of the cardiac lymphatic vessels and the pathological and functional effects upon the heart after interruption of the drainage of cardiac lymph; efficiency in preventing esophageal reflux after replacement of the gastreophageal sphincter with the autotransplanted ileocecal valve; autotransfusion from hemothorax, its effects and safety; coronary blood flow following experimental acute pulmonary embolization; diagnostic value of cardiac scanning and echocardiography for myocardial contusion; hemo-dynamic and neuro functional effects of experimental cross-clamping of the thoracic aorta with or without adjunctive support; experimental pulmonary artery balloon counter-pulsation for the treatment of intraoperative right ventricular failure; effects on the morphological and mechanical properties of the aorta from its wrapping or replacement; mechanism of systemic air embolization following experimental lung injury; pathophysiologic sequelae following experimental papillary muscle ischemia with or without ischemia of the adjacent left ventricular wall, etc. The origins for these investigations were derived from various stimuli. Auto-transfusion from a traumatic hemothorax resulted from the desperate need for the immediate transfusion of many patients with wounds to the heart, great vessels or lungs, which were exsanguinating while we were waiting to procure blood from the blood bank. Others, such as the effects of the ligation of the cardiac lymphatic vessels, came about while we were seeking to understand the mechanism of failing of the heart during the early period of cardiac transplantation. In others such as the cardiac contusion, the thought appeared while we were searching to find a more accurate way to diagnose it. The financial support for the experiments was provided by several agencies including the National Institutes of Health, the Georgia Heart Association, and the Dean's budget for pilot investigative work and from the research budget of our division. The preparation and writing of so many grant applications was laborious and the waiting for their approval was agonizing. All this work was possible because of the close proximity of the hospital operating room and the research laboratory. This made it feasible to do an experiment early in the morning before a scheduled operation in the hospital had started, between cases, or late in the afternoon after the patients' operations were over. More importantly it was possible to carry on all this work because of the great help from the various residents, the lab technicians, my loyal secretary, and the assistance of Dr. Schlant and other collaborators. I am most grateful to all of them.

Carrying on these experiments was most exciting and rewarding. Exciting because we sensed that we were adding a small granule to the colossus building of medicine and rewarding because some of our work resulted in the improvement of care for some patients.

Most all of our studies were presented at national scientific meetings and were published in peer review journals. Speaking in front of the large audience of the American College of Surgeons, the American Heart Association, and the American College of Chest Physicians or to the distinguished members of the Southern Surgical Association or of the American Association for Thoracic Surgeons was an experience mixed with intimidation, fear and pride. Presenting as a junior faculty to everybody and especially to the then giants of Cardiothoracic Surgery was daunting and even frightening during my early years (Figure 14). I both wondered and feared, especially, with my Greek accent, whether my presentation would be understood and whether I would be able to answer the sophisticated and sometimes penetrating questions that would be raised. After the presentation a sense of satisfaction mixed with some pride made my remaining stay at the host city ever more enjoyable.

Figure 14
Photo during an American College of Surgeon meeting.

4. ADMINISTRATIVE DUTIES

In addition to the routine work for the section, my administrative duties consisted of participating in various committees of Grady Memorial Hospital. These included the Operating Room, Respiratory Therapy, Intensive Care, Quality Assurance, and Risk Management committees, etc. as well as various committees of the medical school such as the student admissions, the MD PhD Program, the student research and the medical care research grant awards program committees. In addition, I participated in local and national committees such as the Georgia Heart Research Grant Awarding Committee, etc. This work was time-consuming, but stimulating. It afforded me the opportunity to meet many, great, interesting, and inspiring people.

5. PATIENTS CARE

At the beginning of my career at Emory, the only three institutions in Atlanta that were sporadically doing open-heart surgery were Emory University Hospital, Grady and Saint Joseph hospital. At Emory and at Grady, Dr. Osler Abbott started the programs, and he subsequently was joined by Drs. William Logan and Charles Hatcher, There was only one extracorporeal circulation unit and one pump technician located at Emory and shared by both institutions. When open heart surgery was to be performed at Grady Memorial Hospital, Dr. Abbott, with or without another member of his team, and the pump technician would come to Grady.

For a short period after my arrival we continued sharing both the open-heart unit and the pump technician with Emory. Then, with the help of the Engineering Service, we assembled our own cardiopulmonary bypass unit. It consisted of a homemade frame, DeBakey roller pumps, a disc oxygenator, a bubble trap and a filter. Shortly afterwards, we recruited a pump technician who worked for a while with the Emory technician until she learned the mechanics of the cardiopulmonary bypass unit. From then on, the open heart program at Grady had its own team. At that time, doing an open-heart procedure was a significant project, as it was when I was at Vanderbilt, but this time the responsibility for its outcome rested on my shoulders.

Initially our operating team consisted of a senior cardiothoracic surgical resident, an anesthesiologist, the pump technician and me. None of them then had any reasonable experience in open heart surgery. Also, there was no Intensive Care Unit and no specially trained nurses in the recovery room or anywhere else in the hospital to take care of the post open-heart patients. There were no respiratory therapists and no reasonable respirators.

Therefore, every aspect of perioperative care had to be done or closely supervised by me, a very daunting job. For example, I had to help or supervise the assemblance of the Cardiopulmonary Unit, balance the monitoring equipment and connect the lines to the patient, and watch the induction of anesthesia on the morning of surgery. While we were operating, every so often I had to turn to the pump technician or to the anesthetist to advise, suggest or even sometimes order them to perform certain tasks. Throughout all the open-heart procedure I was greatly concerned and even apprehensive, not so much for my performance, but for how the rest of the team would do theirs. The joy and satisfaction, which I experienced each time a patient was weaned successfully from the cardiopulmonary bypass and was hemodynamically stable, was indescribable.

The disappointment and pain were equally or more indescribable when a patient was slow to come off bypass, and especially when, on rare occasions, the patient's life could not be sustained without cardiopulmonary bypass. There was tremendous sadness when I had to make the decision to stop the pump knowing that the patient would soon expire. On such occasions, even though we had spent numerous exhausting hours in the operating room using every known remedy to sustain the patient's life, telling the technician to stop the pump because we had reached the point of no return was an incredibly painful experience. The disappointment, frustration, helplessness were enormous. The most dreadful and emotionally draining moments, however, were when I faced the family of the deceased patient.

How do you tell someone that his or her loved one has passed away in the operating room? There is no easy way to utter these words. How do you comfort them? How do you ease their pain? There is no easy way to do it. Explaining as clearly as possible the reason for the unfortunate outcome, and sharing fully their sorrow was the only way that I could do it. No matter what risk I quoted to the relatives before the operation and even when they were told that the risk was 70 or 80 percent, each of them, understandably, was still surprised with the outcome and expressed disappointment, sadness, pain, and sometimes, even anger. Experiencing all these increased my disappointment, frustration and pain. An occasional sign of understanding the reasons for the loss by some of the relatives or a whisper of thanks by others was a welcome relief to my great sorrow and disappointment.

I tried not to carry all my tormented feelings outside the hospital but that was not always possible. For the next several days, especially when I was alone or at night, the image of the operation would flash in front of me, followed by numerous questions as to what if we had or had not done this or that. Eventually, after prolonged evaluation and re-evaluation of the event and considerable rationalization, I would try to push all that back in my mind so that I could continue my work.

After the patients left the operating room all the postoperative care was performed by the cardiothoracic resident and me. As I mentioned earlier there were no recovery room nurses who had been even reasonably exposed to the care of open-heart patients. Also, the anesthesiologist left the hospital as soon as the patient was transferred out of the operating room. There was no respiratory therapist to address respiratory problems, no cardiologist to address arrhythmias, and no hematologist to remedy a coagulopathy. All the above complications and many others were frequently present during the early era of cardiac surgery.

At that time the prevailing view among surgeons was that patients who had undergone an operation should have all aspects of their care managed by the surgeon. This concept was extended to our early efforts in cardiac surgery. Several months after my arrival at Grady, I was frustrated trying to manage all postoperative complications coupled with an inability to procure a consultant in a reasonable amount of time, especially at nights and during the weekends. I decided to meet with Dr.

Schlant, the Chief of Cardiology. I told him about the dilemma of post operative management of the open heart patients and suggested that it would be of great benefit to our patients and to his Cardiology Fellows if he would assign one of them to rotate on our service. It would be a good educational experience for them, and they could also promptly assist us in the management of non-surgical cardiac problems such as arrhythmias etc. He thought that this was an excellent idea and after approval from his chairman, Dr. J. Willis Hurst, he assigned one fellow each month to rotate on our service.

A month or so afterwards I was called to the office of the Chairman of the Department of Surgery, Dr. J.D. Martin. After a formal greeting, he said he had heard that I had accepted a cardiology fellow rotating through the Grady Cardiothoracic service and that I had delegated some of the care of open heart patients to him. He stated that the surgeon is the captain of the ship and that it is prudent for him or her to take care of his or her own patients and not let others do it.

I explained to him why and how the rotation of the cardiology fellow on our service came about and added that I knew that the surgeon was the captain of the ship but the cardiac surgical ship is considerably more complicated than that of the other surgical specialties. I explained that the open heart patients frequently developed non-surgical complications that required immediate expert care, which was difficult to obtain on nights and weekends. Therefore, I continued, it would be prudent for us to broaden our cardiac surgical team to include, not only cardiologists but also anesthesiologists, hematologists and the blood bank. After a short pause he stated that, it seemed that I knew what is needed. Therefore he advised me to do whatever was needed to optimize the patients care. Shortly afterwards, the anesthesiology department became more involved with the management of our cardiac surgical patients as did other services, such as hematology etc. and a respiratory therapy unit was soon formed. The incorporation of the above services, as well as the recruitment subsequently of our first physician assistant, Sue Ellen Vlassis, brought our open-heart team to a fairly good level, but it was always still difficult to reach the level which was present in some private institutions.

The anesthesia at those hospitals began to be provided exclusively by anesthesiologists who had taken some additional training in anesthesia for open-heart patients and who devoted all their efforts to the management of these patients. Also, the surgical nurses had been additionally trained and limited their work to open heart surgery. For our anesthesiologists, cardiac anesthesia was a fraction of their total work, providing anesthesia for all other surgical specialties. Our operating room nurses, except for Ruby Wilson initially and Rena Thomas afterwards, were randomly assigned to our operating room and they had very limited, if any, experience in open heart surgery. Ruby, who was with us 25 years, was a very vivacious, high-spirited, pleasant, hardworking lady, who joined our team in the very early days. During all her career she devoted most of her excellent efforts to the intraoperative care of the open heart patients. Similarly, Rena who followed her for the next fifteen years was easygoing, pleasant, relatively quiet, and an unassuming lady. She too, fully assumed Ruby's role and carried it on for the rest of my tenure. It was not terribly unusual, however, for them to be off duty or assigned to another room.

From my point of view, the reasons for any deficiency in Grady's team, in a broad sense, were due to the following factors: the nature of the institution and the public perception about it, its great size, the type of indigent patient that we treated and the financial remuneration of its working force. The public image of Grady, as far as I have experienced it, was that it was an awesome, somewhat rough, very large and intimidating institution. It was also an admirable place for the care that it provided as long as it was provided by someone else and to someone else. Grady was and still is a two-county charity hospital that treats the least privileged citizens of our city and most of the severe injuries in Metropolitan Atlanta. As a result its patients often had multiple medical problems that were difficult to treat. In addition, despite the tasking work at Grady, its working force usually received less compensation than their comrades in the private sector. As a consequence, the turnover of its personnel, nurses, physician assistants, etc was significant.

Over the years numerous medical personnel received their training at Grady. Once they became proficient, they went on to provide excellent care throughout our state, the country and even abroad. Training medical personnel has been the mission and one of Grady's great contributions to society. Nevertheless, this frequent flow of personnel in and out generated both transient and lasting vacuums, which needed to be filled.

To compensate for any shortage that existed or created in our team, the rest of our group stepped in. Having started my professional life at the beginning of cardiac surgery, I learned not to take any chances when it came to patients' care. I carried this motto throughout my career. I delegated tasks to the members of our team according to their abilities. But, even then, either I helped or closely supervised all their work and checked as to whether the task needed to be done, was completed and checked the results.

For each major operation I checked the overall status of the patient and as well as the cohesion and skills of the operating room team. If any component was not what was needed, I tried to alter it and many times succeeded. Whenever such a change could not be done, I tried to strengthen the weak link with my contribution or that of any other member of our team. Not infrequently, we had to oversee and coordinate the pharmacological support of our patients during induction of anesthesia, as well as during and after cardiopulmonary bypass. Similarly, if our scrub nurse was inexperienced, we checked to be sure that she or he had whatever we needed or might need on the instrument table or at immediate reach.

One member of our team that I did not worry about was the perfusionist. This occurred early on when we recruited Ms. Lynn Phender from a newly established perfusionist school and continued after the perfusonists from all Emory affiliated hospitals were integrated. They not only did their job flawlessly, but also gave valuable help whenever it was needed.

With the help of all the members of the cardiac surgical team, the cardiologist, the anesthesiologists, the perfusionist, the respiratory therapists, the physician assistants, the surgical and intensive care room nurses, and especially, our great residents we performed all the established cardiothoracic procedures as well as some novel ones.

In November, 1970, D.McK., a 37-year-old lady was brought to the emergency room with a self-inflicted gunshot wound to her left chest. She was taken immediately to the operating room. The chest was quickly opened, and a 3 by 4 centimeter wound of the anterolateral wall of the left ventricle was found. She was immediately connected to the heart lung machine, and the heart was emptied and stopped. Suturing the wound edges together to close such a large hole of the heart was not possible. Then, after considerable trepidation as to what to do, I recalled Dr. Harold Collins previous work on dogs at Vanderbilt that demonstrated the feasibility of replacing a portion of the left ventricle with Teflon cloth. In desperation and with some relief for thinking of a solution to our dilemma, we closed the hole in the heart by suturing a 4-centimeter by 4.5-centimeter piece of Teflon cloth. While doing that, I worried since the wound edges were badly bruised. Would the suture line hold when the left ventricle was filled with blood and began to contract? Would the function of the heart with part of the heart's left ventricular wall consisting of Teflon cloth be able to sustain her life? Fortunately, to my pleasant surprise, the answers to these questions were positive. What a relief and a joy it was to have her recover from a wound that up to then be thought to be irreparable. The patient lived a long life and had two successful pregnancies. She was the first patient with such a large wound of the heart to be successfully closed with a piece of Teflon3.

Miss S.V., a 14-year-old girl, came to Grady in 1966 complaining of shortness of breath. The tests showed that she had severe leakage of her aortic valve and an aneurysm of the first part of the ascending aorta, the first part of the main tube that allows blood to flow from the heart to the rest of the body. We operated and successfully replaced her aortic valve with a prosthetic one, and replaced the aorta with a Dacron cloth tube. She was seen by Dr. Brian Baldwin, then a cardiology fellow, 26 months later because she began to notice a pulsation of the sternum. Dr. Baldwin presented the case to Dr. Schlant who told him to meet with me and see if we could do anything for Ms. V. Upon my return from a national meeting, Dr. Baldwin came to my office and told me that Ms. V. had come to his clinic complaining of the pulsation. Aortography showed that she had formed a huge aneurysm of the small portion of the aorta between the aortic valve and the Dacron tube of the ascending aorta. He added that Dr. Schalnt wanted to know whether anything could be done about it.

At the national meeting that I had just attended with most of the leading figures in cardiac surgery, the question was raised as to how to manage an aneurysm involving the sinuses of valsalva. The answer was that this problem could be treated by replacing the ascending aorta, after removing the non-coronary sinus down at the level of the aortic valve annulus and removing the other two sinuses down close to the ostia of the coronary arteries. Unfortunately, this technique was not applicable in Ms. V's. case. Therefore, I said, I have no answer to Dr.Schlant's question. He left my office disappointed as I was also for my inability to offer a solution. I tried to forget this patient since I could not do anything for her, but every so often someone would remind me about her. Several days later early in the morning, a thought as to how we could treat Ms. V. came to my mind. I reasoned that we already had considerable experience on how to operate on the coronary arteries. We knew the size of the patient's prosthetic valve and the size of the Dacron graft that we had previously implanted in her. Therefore, before we stopped the heart we could first suture a new valve to the end of a similar sized new Dacron tube. Then, after we took out her current valve, the end of the new Dacron tube containing the new valve would be sutured to the site of the removed valve and the other end of the tube would be sutured to the previously placed Dacron tube. Finally, after that was completed, we could manage the coronary arteries by either implanting their aortic orifices into the Dacron tube or by ligating, and then bypassing them with a piece of vein. I became so excited with my revelation that I could not sleep for the rest of the night. The next morning I walked into Dr. Schlant's office and told him about my thoughts as to how we could possibly remedy Ms. V.'s problem. He thought that my idea was sound and suggested that I should present it to Ms. V. and her family. Thereafter, I presented the problem and my proposed solution to Dr. Charles Hatcher. He became excited and agreed that my plan was sound and even offered to come to Grady and to scrub with me during surgery. I then met with the patient and her father and explained that up to that time, unfortunately, there was no known operation as to how to treat her illness.

I told them that I had a novel and untested idea as how to manage the problem. I offered no guarantee about its outcome, but I thought that it should work. I explained that it would be very difficult and risky, but, if they agreed, I would be willing to go ahead with my plan.

Although they had been previously told that her aneurysm could burst at any time causing her instant death, they said that they would like to think about the operation and then decide. I agreed with them that it was a major and difficult decision and that it was prudent not to rush. With at least a trace of hope, they told me they would let me know about their decision at a later date.

My emotions about my proposed venture were mixed. I was excited to do this novel procedure since this was the only reasonable alternative, but I feared the outcome. The magnitude of the operation was horrendous, the risk quite significant, the outcome unknown, and, yet, there was no other choice for this young patient. I kept second-guessing myself. Was it right for me to even suggest it? What if this or that went wrong and indeed there were plenty of things that could go wrong? I, however, comforted my anxiety and fear with the belief that they would choose not to go on with the operation. This comforting unfortunately was interrupted when later the patient with her father came to my office and said "You did the first operation successfully and we trust you to do this one, even though it had not been done before." I was flattered and stunned with their statement at the same time.

A few days later, with everything planned meticulously and with Dr. Hatcher on board, we operated on her. As expected, the operation was tedious, difficult, and very long, but it went as we had planned it. The fatigue and tension of everyone who labored from 8 o'clock in the morning until 4 o'clock in the afternoon was replaced with great relief when the patient was wheeled out of the operating room.

We believed then that this was the first patient in whom such an operation had been performed. Later on, when we began the preparation for its publication, we discovered that this procedure was previously done.

So, it turned out to be the third such case rather than the first. Nevertheless, my satisfaction as well as that of my colleagues, was not diminished. This event, however, affirmed the dogma that it should never be assumed that an idea was new and had not been reported or a procedure had not been done until the literature was thoroughly researched. I practiced that dogma when at Vanderbilt I conceived the project on "portal vein grafting." But on this occasion I assumed that if none of the giants of cardiac surgery who were present at the meeting I attended had an opinion as how to manage Ms. V.'s problem, then it had not been reported or attempted.

During my long years as a cardiac surgeon the field of open-heart surgery continued to improve exponentially. The tireless and painstaking efforts of all of our colleagues led to the development and perfection of surgical procedures for the management of almost all of the diseases of the heart. Similarly, their constant probing and researching as to the causes for all the ill effects of the extracorporeal circulation resulted in eliminating some of them, and minimizing and satisfactorily treating others. Overtime, industry developed, more efficient, safer and more inert component of the heart lung machine. All these forces, in concert, resulted in making open heart surgery safe, relatively easy and enjoyable.

The early years of my career were full of excitement and fear. Excitement because everything we did was relatively new and fear because its outcome was unpredictable. As time passed the progress that I just mentioned made open heart surgery as safe and as predictable as all other old surgical procedures. I very much enjoyed the challenge, growth and even the pain of my early years of cardiac surgery. During my later years I equally or more enjoyed the fruits of the earlier hard work by many distinguished investigators which made open heart surgery safe and predictable.

As the years went by the number of patients operated upon at Grady Memorial Hospital progressively increased and for the last 30 years the volume has remained relatively steady. Most of these patients had a cardiac disease in its extreme form, and each one of them frequently had multiple other problems as well. As a result the operations were challenging and risky, but very instructive for our residents. We performed thousands of operations over the entire spectrum of cardiac and general thoracic surgery. Some were old, some new, and two[3,4] not done before.

Also, as was mentioned earlier, we contributed to the training of more than 120 residents who became admirable cardiothoracic surgeons. When they began their rotation with me at Grady they were not quite sure of themselves much like baby eagles almost ready to fly away but reluctant to take off. It was a gratifying experience to nurture and observe them day after day as they grew more confident, and by the end of their rotation, became ready to soar. All of them have been and will continue to provide excellent cardiothoracic surgical care throughout our country and abroad, and some of them have made noticeable contributions in our field. I am proud of each of them. Also, I thank them on behalf of myself and the thousands of our patients for their contributions to fulfill our most important mission at Grady by providing cardiothoracic surgical care to the least privileged citizens of our city. This was carried out uninterruptedly for the last 43 years, a record that very few, if any, similar institutions could claim.

Our secretaries and our physician assistants recorded all of our surgical experience at Grady Memorial Hospital. This made it possible to periodically review it, report to national meetings, and to publish over 170 articles in peer reviewed journals, over 70 book chapters, and three books, also. I would like to express my gratitude to both my dedicated secretary, Jerry Brown, and to my physician assistant, Sue Ellen Vlasis Hale, for their hard work and for their innumerable contributions to my publications.

Finally, I want to especially thank my current secretary, Brenda Ramseur, without whose prompt, efficient, and unselfish work it would have been very difficult to complete this text. I am grateful to her for her dedication and tireless typing and retyping of this biography. Above all, I am most thankful for her kindness and pleasantness, which made the last 7 years of my career flow easily and pleasantly.

The open heart program at the Atlanta Veteran's Administration Hospital was started a few years after I joined the Emory Faculty. Not long afterwards, it was stopped for the same reasons that it was stopped in several similar and city charity hospitals. Later on, it was restarted and I was asked to contribute part of my time to that service. I worked there two days of the week, Tuesdays and Thursdays when no elective surgery was performed at Grady. Initially, I shared the open-heart cases with Dr. Sink. When Dr. Sink left and until Dr. Vega was recruited my team and I carried out all the open heart surgical workload. My almost 30 years of work there was a considerable strain to me. I did however derive great satisfaction from contributing to the VA open heart program and for keeping it going when there was no other cardiac surgeon available to sustain it.

Finally, after almost 43 years of tenure at Emory University, I retired on March, 2007, with some sadness and great satisfaction. Although I was blessed to be able to work much longer than most of my colleagues, leaving a service that I had developed and sustained it during those long, challenging and sometimes difficult years felt as though I was separating from my own children.

The work was hard and sometimes despairing, but it had been most rewarding. To have the opportunity to contribute to the development of over 120 cardiothoracic surgeons, to make my small contributions to the field of medicine, and, most importantly, to provide cardiothoracic surgical care to the least privileged patients of our city over all those years, has been a humbling experience. I am grateful to Emory University for giving me the opportunity to be a small part of it and to Grady Memorial Hospital for its trust and support.

Also, I could not have safely and to some degree successfully traveled this long road without the help of the many people that I have previously mentioned. In addition, the love, understanding, and guidance of my three sons, Drs. Nikolas, Peter, and John, and above all my wife, Hytho's love, support, comfort, and encouragement have been the greatest gifts of my life over our 42 years of being together. My deepest gratitude to her, to all my family and to my colleagues for allowing me to pursue my profession with great joy and satisfaction (Figure 15).

Figure 15
Photo during the retirement party which was given by the Department of Surgery and the Cardiothoracic Section of Emory School of Medicine.

This long trip leads me to conclude that life is a journey in the open sea. Sometimes, it is full of beauty, joy, excitement, and inspiration. At other times it is calm and even boring. The rest of the time it is stormy, full of worries, anxieties, fears, and even dangers. Therefore, enjoying life when times are good and navigate carefully when times are bad, always remaining focused as to where we wanted to go, confer the best chance to reach the desired destination.

PART C

REFERENCES:

1. The autobiography of Benjamin Franklin; New York, Buccaneer Books, Inc. (International Standard Book Number: 0-89966-416-41), page 6, Copyright 1984.

2. George C. Papavizas: Blood and tears. Greece 1940-1949. A story of war and love. Published in 2002 by American Hellenic Institute Foundation, 1220 16th Street NW, Washington, DC 20036. Pages 80-81.

3. Harris B. Schumacher, Jr. The evolution of cardiac surgery. Indiana University Press, Bloomington, Indianapolis, 1992. Page 180.

4. Panagiotis N Symbas et al. Traumtic rupture of the aortic arch between left common carotid and left subclavian arteries and avulsion of the left subclavian artery. Annals of Surgery 170: 152-156. 1969.

APPENDIX

CURRICULUM VITAE

NAME: Panagiotis N Symbas, MD
DATE AND PLACE BIRTH: August 15, 1925 Greece
EDUCATION: Gymnasium of Kastoria, Greece 1954
MD University

INTERNSHIP & RESIDENCES:
1956-1957   Vanderbilt University, Nashville, Tennessee (Surgery Internship)
1957-1960   Vanderbilt University, Nashville, Tennessee (Surgery, Jr. Asst. Resident)
1960-1961   Vanderbilt University, Nashville, Tennessee (Surgery Chief Resident)

POSTDOCTORAL FELLOWSHIP:
1962-1963   Louis University, St. Louis, Missouri (Fellow, Cardiovascular Surgery)

ACADEMIC APPOINTMENTS:
2007-Present Emory University School of Medicine, Atlanta, GA (Professor Emeritus of Cardiothoracic Surgery)
1973-2007   Emory University School of Medicine, Atlanta, GA (Professor of Cardiothoracic Surgery)

PANAGIOTIS N. SYMBAS

1968-1973   Emory University School of Medicine, Atlanta, GA (Associate Professor Surgery)
1970-1984   Emory University School of Medicine, Atlanta, GA (Director, Daniel C Elkin Surgical Research Laboratory)
1966-1968   Emory University School of Medicine, Atlanta, GA (Assistant Professor of Surgery)
1964-1965.1 Emory University School of Medicine, Atlanta, GA (Associate in Thoracic Surgery)
1964-2007   Grady Memorial Hospital, Atlanta, GA (Director, Thoracic/Cardiovascular Surgery Division)
1961-1962   Vanderbilt University, Nashville, Tennessee (Instructor)

BOARD CERTIFICATIONS AND DATES:
3/19/1963   American Board of Surgery
11/3/1963   Board of Thoracic Cardiovascular Surgery

PROFESSIONAL SOCIETIES:
   Fellow, The American Surgical Association
   Member, The Society of University Surgeons
   Member, The American Association for Thoracic Surgery
   Member, Society of Thoracic Surgeons
   Member, The Society for Vascular Surgeons
   Member, The Association of Academic Surgery
   Member, American Federation for Clinical Research
   Member, The International Society of University Surgeons
   Member, The American Association of Cardiovascular Surgery, North American Chapter
   Member, American College of Surgeons
   Member, American College of Cardiology
   Member, American College of Chest Physicians
   Member, American Medical Association
   Member, The Southeastern Surgical Congress
   Member, Southern Medical Association
   Member, American Heart Association

Member, Georgia Thoracic Society
Member, Societe Internationale de Chirugie
Member, The Georgia Surgical Society
Member, Honorary, The Hellenic Surgical Congress
Member, Honorary of the Hellenic Congress of Thoracic, Cardiac & Vascular Surgery

BIBLIOGRAPHY

PN Symbas, MD

Articles

1. Chamberlain NO, Symbas PN, Foster IH, Harris AP: The Influence of Infrarenal Aortic Cross—Clamping on Renal Blood Flow. Surg Forum 11:501-503, 1960.
2. Symbas PN, Killen DA, Scott HW Jr: Regulation of Gastric Emptying of Gastroduodenal Interposition of the Ileocecal Sphincter Following Ablation of the Pylorus. Surg Forum11:320-321, 1960.
3. Killen DA, Symbas PN, Burrus G, Scott HW Jr: Use of the Transposed Ileocecal Valve for Sphincteric Control of Gastric Emptying After Ablation of the Pylorus. Surgery 48:838-845 (Nov), 1960.
4. Classen KL, Wiederanders RE, Symbas PN Meckel's Diverticulum Associated with Carcinoid Tumor. Surgery 49:328-333 (Mar), 1961.
5. Symbas PN, Foster JH, Scott HW Jr: Experimental Vein Grafting in the Portal Venous System. Surgery 50:97-106 (Jul), 1961.
6. Symbas PN, Scott HW Jr, Diveley WL: Experimental Studies of Intrapleural Injection of Sodium Heparin in Pneumonectomized Dogs With and Without Infection. J Thorac Cardiovasc Surg 42:213-218 (Aug), 1961.

7. Symbas PN, Byrd BF Jr, Johnson JS, Younger R, Foster JH: Influence of Hypothermia on Pancreatic Function. Ann Surg 154:509-515 (Oct), 1961.
8. Symbas PN, Byrd BF Jr, Johnson JS, Younger R, Foster JH: Influence of Body Temperature Variations on Pancreatic Function. Surg Forum 12:364-366, 1961.
9. Killen DA, Symbas PN, Scott HW Jr: The Effects of Prolonged Exposure of the Mucosa of the Ileocecum to Gastric Chyme. J Tenn Med Assoc 55:135-139 (Apr), 1962.
10. Symbas PN, Woods LP, Collins HA: Changes in Cerebrospinal Fluid Pressure Following Experimental Superior Vena Cava and Right Pulmonary Artery Shunt. J Thorac Cardiovasc Surg 44:628-633 (Nov), 1962.
11. Symbas PN, Foster JH, Scott HW Jr: Late Behavior of Portal Vein Grafts. Surg Forum 13:322-324, 1962.
12. Killen DA, Symbas PN: Effect of Preservation of Pyloric Sphincter During Antrectomy on Postoperative Gastric Emptying. Am J Surg 104:836-842 (Dec), 1962.
13. Diveley WL, Symbas PN, Scott HW Jr, Daniel RA Jr: Compression of Trachea and Esophagus by Congenital Vascular Anomalies. South Med J 56:1-10 (Jan), 1963.
14. Foster JH, Atkins RB, Chamberlain NO, Symbas PN, Harris AP: The Renal Effects of Lower Abdominal Aortic Cross-Clamping: Report of Negative Results in Dogs and Monkeys. JAMA 183:451-454 (Feb), 1963.
15. Symbas PN, Scott HW Jr: Traumatic Aneurysm of the Pulmonary Artery. J Thorac Cardiovasc Surg 45:645-649 (May), 1963.
16. OrNeill JA Jr, Symbas PN: Femoral Hernia Complicated by Strangulation of a Meckel's Diverticulum. J Term Med Assoc 56:172-174 (May), 1963.
17. Symbas PN, Killen DA, Scott HW Jr: An Experimental Study of the Effects of Altering Size of Gastric Pouch and Integrity of Pyloric Sphincter on Gastric Emptying. Surg Gynecol Obstet 116:643-646 (Jun), 1963.

18. Hanlon CR, Willman VL, Mudd JG, Symbas PN, Cooper T: Closed Valvotomy for Pulmonary Valvar Stenosis. Arch Surg 86:887-890 (Jun), 1963.
19. Symbas PN, Cooper T, Gantner GA Jr, Willman VL: Lymphatic Drainage of the Heart:Effects of Experimental Interruption of Lymphatic Vessels. Surg Forum 14:254-256, 1963.
20. Sawyers IL, Symbas PN, Stephenson SE Jr: Cyclophosphamide in the Treatment of Disseminated Neuroblastoma. Am Surg 30:182-187 (Mar), 1964.
21. Symbas PN, Puaya FA, Scott HW Jr: Malabsorption Syndrome Secondary to Jejunal Stenosis and Incomplete Rotation of Colon. Ann Surg 159:574-580 (Apr), 1964.
22. Symbas PN, Jellinek M, Cooper T, Hanlon CR: Effect of Hyperthermia on Plasma Catecholamines and Histamine. Arch Tnt Pharmacodyn Ther 150:132-136 (Jul), 1964.
23. Willman VL, Hanlon CR, Symbas PN, Kelly JJ, Mudd JG: Evaluation of Cardiac Function by Suprasternal Puncture. J Thorac Cardiovasc Surg 48:959-963 (Dec), 1964.
24. Wiliman VL, Symbas PN, Mamiya RT, Cooper T, Hanlon CR: Unusual Aspects of Intracavitary Tumors of the Heart. Report of Two Cases. Dis Chest 47:669-671 (Jun), 1965.
25. Foster IH, Jolly PC, Symbas PN, Diveley WL: Vein Grafting in Portal Venous System. Arch Surg 91:716-724 (Nov), 1965.
26. Cho YW, Symbas PN: Effect of Prolonged Cardiac Lymphatic Ligation and Endogenous Histamine on the Cardiac Mitochondrial and Myosin Enzymes in Dogs. Life Sci 4:1461—1466, 1965.
27. Symbas PN, Cooper T, Gantner GE Jr, Wiliman VL: Lymphatics of the Heart. Anatomic Effects Following Interruption of the Drainage of the Cardiac Lymph. Arch Path 81:573-575(Jun), 1966.
28. Symbas PN, Logan WD Jr, Hatcher CR Jr, Abbott OA: Factors in the Successful Recognition and Management of Esophageal Perforation. South Med J 59:1090-1096 (Sept), 1966.
29. Hatcher CR Jr, Abbott OA, Logan WD Jr, Symbas PN: Current Status of Thymectomy for Myasthenia Gravis. Ann Thorac Surg 3:132-135 (Feb), 1967.

30. Symbas PN, Aydin K, and Abbott OA: Replacement of the Cardioesophageal Sphincter with the Ileocecal Valve. Dis Chest 51:125-132 (Feb), 1967.
31. Symbas PN, Schlant RC, Hatcher CR Jr, Lindsay J: Congenital Fistula of Right Coronary Artery to Right Venticle;Complications by Actinobacillus Actinomycetemcomitans Endacateritis. J Thorac Cardiovasc Surg 53:379-384 (Mar), 1967
32. Symbas PN, Schiant RC, Logan WD Jr, Lindsay J, MacCannell K, Zakaryia M: Traumatic Aorticopulmonary Fistula Complicated by Postoperative Low Cardiac Output Treated with Dopamine. Ann Surg 165:614-619 (Apr), 1967.
33. Logan WD Jr, Hatcher CR Jr, Symbas PN, Abbott OA: Additional Consideration in Pulmonary Embolectomy. Am Surg 33:706-710 (Sept), 1967.
34. Symbas PN, Abbott OA, Leonard J: The Effects of Artificial Ventilation on Cerebrospinal Fluid Pressure. J Thorac Cardiovasc Surg 54:126-131, 1967.
35. Symbas PN, Abbott OA, Ende N: Surgical Stress and Its Effects on Serum Cholesterol. Surgery 61:22 1-227, 1967.
36. Symbas PN, Exarhos ND, Preininger RE, Kent KM, and Ojeda OP: Coronary Sinus Blood Flow Following Pulmonary Embolus. Surg Forum 18:108-109, 1967.
37. Symbas PN: Indirect Method of Extraction of Foreign Body of the Esophagus. Ann Surg167:78-80 (Jan), 1968.
38. Symbas PN, Parr JA: Early Surgical Treatment for Acute Pneumococcal Aortic Valvulitis with Aortic Insufficiency, Acquired Ventricular Septal Defect and Aortico-Right Ventricular Shunt. Ann Surg 167:580-585 (Apr), 1968.
39. Symbas PN, Abbott OA, Hatcher CR Jr, Logan WD Jr: Abnormal Congenital Coronary Arterial Communications. Am Rev Respir Dis 97:1104-1111 (Jun), 1968.
40. Symbas PN, Hatcher CR Jr, Mansour KA: Projectile Embolus of the Lung. J Thorac Cardiovasc Surg 56:97-103 (Jul), 1968.
41. Hatcher CR Jr, Calvert JR. Logan WD Jr, Symbas PN, Abbott OA: Prolonged Endothracheal Intubation. Surg Gynecol & Obstet 172:759-762 (Oct),1968.

42. Wimberly JE, Symbas PN, Foster JH: Portal Vein Grafts: Microscopic Study after a Seven Year Follow-up. Surgery 64:761-762 (Oct), 1968.
43. Symbas, PN, Schlant RC, Gravanis MB: Total Interruption of the Cardiac Lymphatics: Functional and Pathologic Effects. Surg Forum 19:169-171, 1968.
44. Hatcher CR Jr, Symbas PN, Logan WD Jr, Abbott OA: Surgical Aspects of Endocarditis of the Aortic Root. Am J Cardiol 23:192-198 (Feb), 1969.
45. Symbas PN: (A Collaborative Study): Preoperative Irradiation of Cancer of the Lung. Preliminary Report of a Therapeutic Trial. Cancer 23:419-430 (Feb), 1969.
46. Symbas PN, Hatcher CR Jr, Abbott OA, Logan WD Jr: An Appraisal of Pulmonary Sequestration. Special Emphasis on Unusual Manifestations. Am Rev Respir Dis 99:406-414 (Mar), 1969.
47. Symbas PN, Walter PF, Hurst JW, Schiant RC: Fenestration of Aortic Cups Causing Aortic Regurgitation. J Thorac Cardiovasc Surg 57:464-470 (Apr), 1969.
48. Symbas PN, Schlant RC, Gravanis MB, Shepherd RL: Pathologic and Functional Effects of the Heart Following Interruption of the Cardiac Lymph Drainage. J Thorac Cardiovasc Surg 57:577-584 (Apr), 1969.
49. Hatcher CR Jr, Logan WD Jr, Symbas PN, Talley RC, Abbott OA: The Current Role of Surgery for Pulmonary Embolism. South Med J 62:567-572 (May), 1969.
50. Symbas PN, Levin JM, Fen-ier FL, Sybers RG: A study of Autotransfusion from Hemothorax. South Med J 62:671-674 (June), 1969.
51. Symbas PN, Pourhamidi A, Levin JM: Traumatic Rupture of the Aortic Arch Between Left Common Carotid and Left Subclavian Arteries and Avulsion of the Left Subclavian Artery. Ann Surg 170:152-156 (Jul), 1969.
52. Abbott OA, Mansour KA, Logan WD Jr, Hatcher CR Jr, Symbas PN: A traumatic so—called "Spontaneous" Rupture of the Esophagus: A Review of 47 Personal Cases with Comments on

a New Method of Surgical Therapy. J Thorac Cardiovasc Surg 59:67-83 (Jan), 1970.
53. Symbas PN, Logan WI) Jr, Vakil HC: Granular Cell Myoblastoma of the Bronchus. Long—term Follow-up after Its Local Resection. Ann Thorac Surg 9:136-142 (Feb), 1970.
54. Talley RC, Baldwin BJ, Symbas PN, Nutter DO: Right Atrial Myxoma. Unusual Presentation with Cyanosis and Clubbing. Am J Med 48:256-260 (Feb), 1970.
55. Hatcher CR Jr, Mansour K, Logan WD Jr, Symbas PN, Abbott OA: Surgical Complications of Myocardial Infarction. Am Surg 36:163-170 (Mar), 1970.
56. Symbas PN, Sehdeva JS: Penetrating Wounds of the Thoracic Aorta. Ann Surg 71:441-450 (Mar), 1970.
57. Symbas PN, Baldwin BJ, Silverman ME, Galambos JT: Marfan's Syndrome with Aneurysm of Ascending Aorta and Aortic Regurgitation. Surgical Treatment and New Histochemical Observations. Am J Cardiol 25:483-489 (Apr), 1970.
58. Underwood FO, Sybers RG, Ferrier FL, Symbas PN: Cine-Angiographic Studies of the Pathophysiologic Sequelae of Experimental Papillary Muscle Damage in Dogs. Am J Roentgenol, Rad Therapy and Nuclear Med 108:702-707 (Apr), 1970.
59. Symbas PN, Sehdeva JS, Abbott OA, Hatcher CR Jr, Logan WD Jr: Penetrating Wounds of the Thoracic Aorta and Great Arteries. South Med J 63:853-857 (Jul), 1970.
60. Symbas PN, Bonanno JA: Coronary Blood Flow in Acute Experimental Pulmonary Embolization. J Surg Res 10:377-384 (Aug), 1970.
61. Hatcher Cr Jr, Sehdeva J, Waters WC ifi, Shuize V, Logan WI) Jr, Symbas PN, and Abbott OA: Primary Pulmonary Cryptoco—ccosis. J Thorac Cardiovasc Surg 6 1:39-48 (Jan), 1971.
62. Symbas PN, Shuford WH, Edwards FK, Sehdeva JS: Vascular Ring: Persistent Right Aortic Arch, Patent Proximal Left Arch, Obliterated Distal Left Arch, and Left Ligamentum Arteriosum. J Thorac Cardiovasc Surg 61:149-153 (Jan),1971

63. SymbasPN: Penetrating Wounds of the Heart. J Med Assoc Ga 60:53-54 (Feb), 1971.
64. Symbas PN: Non-Penetrating Wounds of the Heart and Great Vessels. J Med Assoc Ga 60:95-96(Mar), 1971.
65. Symbas PN, Abbott OA, Logan WD, Hatcher CR Jr: Atrial Myxomas: Special Emphasis on Unusual Manifestations. Chest 59:504-5 10 (May), 1971.
66. Hatcher CR Jr, Symbas PN, Logan WI) Jr, Mansour KA, Abbott OA: Surgical Management of Complications of Bacterial Endocarditis. Ann Surg 173:1045-1052 (Jun), 1971.
67. Symbas PN, Nugent JT, Abbott OA, Logan WD Jr, Hatcher CR Jr: Nontuberculous Pleural Empyema in Adults. The Role of a Modified Eloesser Procedure in Its Management. Ann Thorac Surg 12:69-78 (Jul), 1971.
68. Hatcher CR Jr, Logue RB, Logan WI) Jr, Symbas PN, Mansour KA, Abbott OA: Pericardiectomy for recurrent pericarditis. J Thorac Cardiovasc Surg 62:371-378 (Sept), 1971.
69. Symbas PN, Jacobs WF, Schlant RC: Chronic Pulmonary Arterial Embolization or Thrombosis. Am J Cardiol 28:342-347 (Sept), 1971.
70. Symbas PN, Baldwin BJ, Schlant RC, Hurst JW: Unusual complications ofBacterial Endocarditis. Br Heart J 33:664-670 (Sept), 1971.
71. Symbas PN, Raizner AE, Tyras DH, Hatcher CR Jr, Inglesby TV, Baldwin BJ: Aneurysms ofAll Sinuses of Valsalva in Patients with Marfan's Syndrome: An Unusual Late Complication Following Replacement of Aortic Valve and Ascending Aorta for Aortic Regurgitation and Fusiform Aneurysm of Ascending Aorta. Ann Surg 174:902-907 (Dec), 1971.
72. Symbas PN, Galambos JT, Sybers RG: Experimental Left Atrial Thrombus and Human Atrial Myxoma. J Surg Res 12:8-16 (Jan), 1972.
73. Symbas PN, Tyras DH, McCraw DB: Repair of a Left Ventricular Traumatic Defect with a Dacron Prothesis. J Thorac Cardiovasc Surg 63:608-612 (Apr), 1972.

74. Mazyck EM, Bonner JT, Herd HM, Symbas PN: Pulmonary Lavage for Childhood Pulmonary Alveolar Proteinosis. J Pediat 80:839-842 (May), 1972.
75. Symbas PN, Tyras DH, Hatcher CR Jr, Perry B: Penetrating Wounds of the esophagus. Ann Thorac Surg 13:552-558 (Jun), 1972.
76. Kassanoff I, Symbas PN, Wenger NK: Ventricular Demand Pacemaker Inhibition by an Atrial Fixed Rate Pacemaker. Chest 62:346-348 (Sept), 1972.
77. Symbas PN, Ware RE, Belenkie I, Nutter DO: Traumatic Biventricular Pseudoaneurysm of the Heart with Venticular Septal Defect. J Thorac Cardiovasc Surg 64:647-65 1 (Oct), 1972.
78. Symbas PN: Autotransfusion from Hemothorax: Experimental and Clinical Studies. J Trauma12:689-695, 1972.
79. Ware RE, Martin LG, Tyras DH, Kourias E, Symbas PN: Coronary Arterial Injection of Radioactive Albumin Microspheres in Diagnosis of Experimental Myocardial Contusion. Surg Forum 23:138-139, 1972.
80. Symbas PN, Tyras DH, Ware RE, Hatcher CR Jr: Rupture of the Aorta: A Diagnostic Triad. Ann Thorac Surg 15:405-410 (Apr), 1973.
81. Martin LG, Larose JH, Sybers RG, Tyras DH, Symbas PN: myocardial PerfusionImaging with 99m Tc-Albumin Microspheres. Radiology 107:367-370 (May), 1973.
82. Symbas PN, Ware RE: A Syndrome of Defects of the Thoracoabdominal Wall, Diaphragm, Pericardium, and Heart. One-Stage Surgical Repair and Analysis of the Syndrome. J Thorac Cardiovasc Surg 65:914-919 (Jun), 1973.
83. Symbas PN, Tyras DH, Ware RE, DiOrio DA: Traumatic Rupture of the Aorta. Aim Surg 178:6-12 (Jul), 1973.
84. Belenkie I, Carr M, Schlant RC, Nutter DO, Symbas PN: Malfunction of a Cutter-Smeloff Mitral Ball Valve Prosthesis: Diagnosis by Phonocardiography and Echocardiography. Am Heart J 86:399-403 (Sept), 1973.

85. Symbas PN, Tyras DH, Baldwin BJ; Left Ventricular Function During Acute Ethanol Intoxication and Hemodialysis. J Surg Res 15:207-211 (Sept), 1973.
86. Symbas PN, DiOrio DA, Tyras DH, Ware RE, Hatcher CR Jr: Penetrating Cardiac Wounds. Significant Residual and Delayed Sequelae. J Thorac Cardiovasc Surg 66:526-532 (Oct), 1973.
87. Tyras DH, DiOrio DA, Stone RH, Symbas PN: Autotransfusion of Intraperitoneal Blood: An Experimental Study. Am Surg 39:652-656 (Nov), 1973.
88. Symbas PN, Ware RE, DiOrio DA, Hatcher CR Jr: Purulent Pericarditis: A Review of Diagnostic and Surgical Principles. South Med J 67:46-48 (Jan), 1974.
89. Symbas PN, Kourias E, Tyras DH, Hatcher CR Jr: Penetrating Wounds of the Great Vessels. Ann Surg 179:757-762 (May), 1974.
90. Symbas PN: Residual or Delayed Lesions from Penetrating Cardiac Wounds. Chest 66:408-410 (Oct),1974.
91. Symbas PN: Surgical Anatomy of the Great Arteries of the Thorax. Surg Clin N Am 54:1303-1312 (Dec), 1974.
92. Symbas PN: Great Vessel Injury from Penetrating Trauma. J Cardiovasc Surg (Special issue) 620-625, 1975.
93. Symbas PN: Preoperative Irradiation of Cancer of the Lung: Final Report of a Therapeutic Trial. A Collaborative Study. Cancer 36:914-925, 1975.
94. Waldo WJ, Harlaftis NN, Symbas PN: Systemic Air Embolism: Does it Occur After Experimental Penetrating Lung Injury. J Thorac Cardiovasc Surg 71:96-101(Jan), 1976.
95. Symbas PN, Ware RE, Hatcher CR Jr, Temesy-Armos PN: An Operation for Relief of Severe Left Ventricular Outflow Tract Obstruction. J Thorac Cardiovasc Surg 71:245-249 (Feb), 1976.
96. Mansour KA, Symbas PN, Jones EL, Hatcher CR Jr: A Combined Surgical Approach in the Management of Achalasia of the Esophagus. Am Surg 42:192-195 (Mar), 1976.

97. Symbas PN, Harlaftis N, Waldo WJ: Penetrating Cardiac Wounds: A Comparison of Different Therapeutic Methods. Ann Surg 183:377-381 (Apr),1976.
98. Symbas PN, Hatcher CR Jr, Gravanis MB: Myxoma of the Heart: Clinical and Experimental Observations. Ann Surg 183:470-475 (May),1976.
99. Fleming WH, Umstott CE, Symbas PN, Mansour KA, Hatcher CR Jr: The Embryology and Management of Vascular Rings. South Med J 69:878-880 (Jul), 1976.
100. Symbas PN: Cardiac Trauma. Am Heart J 92:387-396 (Sept), 1976.
101. Bloch WN Jr, Felner IM, Wickliffe C, Symbas PN, Schlant RC: Echocardiogram of the Porcine Aortic Bioprosthesis in the Mitral Position. Am J Cardiol 3 8:293-298 (Sept),1976.
102. Bloch WN Jr, Felner JM, Wickliffe C, Symbas PN: Echocardiographic Diagnosis of Thrombus on a Heterograft Aortic Valve in the Mitral Position. Chest 70:399-401 (Sept),1976.
103. Symbas PN, Hatcher CR Jr, Boehm GAW: Acute Penetrating Tracheal Trauma. Ann Thorac Surg 22:473-477 (Nov),1976.
104. Coleman J, Gonzalez A, Harlaftis N, Symbas PN: Myocardial Contusion: Diagnostic Value of Cardiac Scanning and Echocardiography. Surg Forum 27:293-294, 1976.
105. Symbas PN, Harlaffis N: Bullet Emboli in the Pulmonary and Systemic Arteries. Ann Surg185:318-320 (Mar), 1977.
106. Symbas PN: Great Vessel Injury. Am Heart J 93:518-522 (Apr),1977.
107. Harlaftis N, Gonzalez AC, Waldo WJ, Symbas PN: Value of Perfusion Lung Scans in Selection of Patients for Vena Cava Interruption. Chest 7 1:680-682 (May),1977.
108. Gonzalez AC, Waldo W, Harlaftis N, Gravanis M, Symbas PN: Imaging of Experimental Myocardial Contusion: Observations and Pathologic Correlations. Am J Roentgenol128:1039-1040 (Jun),1977.

109. Smiley WH, Gilbert CA, Symbas PN: Bleeding, Clotting and Functional Disability Following Beall Prosthetic Mitral Valve Replacement. South Med 70:801-805 (Jul), 1977.
110. Symbas PN, Hatcher CR Jr, Waldo W: Diaphgragmatic Eventration in Infancy and Childhood. Ann Thorac Surg 24:113-119 (Aug), 1977.
111. Waters DD, Clark DW, Symbas PN, Schlant RC: Aortic and Mitral Valve Replacement in a Patient with Osteogenesis Imperfecta. Chest 72:363-364 (Sept), 1977.
112. Bloch WN, Felner JM, Schlant RC, Symbas PN, Jones EL: The Echocardiogram of the Porcine Aortic Bioprothesis in the Aortic Position. Chest 72:640-646 (Nov), 1977.
113. Sotus PC, Majmudar B, Symbas PN: Carcinoma in Situ of the Esophagus. JAMA 239:335-336 (Jan), 1978.
114. Symbas PN, Harlaftis N, Gonzalez AC: Diagnosis of Pulmonary Embolism: Correlation of Value of Perfusion Lung Scan and Pulmonary Arteriography in Selecting Patients for Inferior Vena Cava Interruption. Am Surg 44:137-142 (Mar), 1978.
115. Faruqui AMA, Maloy WC, Felner JM, Schiant RC, Logan WD, Symbas PN: Symptomatic Myocardial Bridging of Coronary Artery. Am J Cardiol 41:1305-1310 (Jun), 1978.
116. Symbas PN, Hatcher CR Jr, Harlaftis N: Spontaneous Rupture of the Esophagus. Ann Surg187:634-640,Jun, 1978.
117. Symbas PN: Blunt Traumatic Rupture of the Diaphragm. Ann Thorac Surg 26:193-194 (Sept), 1978.
118. Symbas PN: Extraoperative Autotransfusion from Hemothorax. Surgery 84:722-727 (Nov),1978.
119. Bloch WN, Karcioglu Z, Felner JM, Miller JS, Symbas PN, Schiant RC: Idiopathic Perforation of a Porcine Aortic Bioprosthesis in the Aortic Position. Chest 74:579-59 1 (Nov),1978.
120. Meier GH, Symbas PN: Systemic Air Embolization: Factors Involved in Its Production Following Penetrating Lung Injury. Am Surg 44:765-77 1(Dec), 1978.
121. Symbas PN: Acute Traumatic Hemothorax. Ann Thorac Surg 26:195-196, 1978.

122. Felner JM, Arensburg D, Meyer TP, Symbas PN, Schlant RC: Ventricular Septal Rupture and Mitral Regurgitation in a Patient with an Acute Myocardial Infarction. Chest 75:614-617 (May), 1979.
123. Meier GH, Wood WJ, Symbas PN: Systemic Air Embolization from Penetrating Lung Injury. Ann Thorac Surg27:161-168 (Feb),1979.
124. Mansour KA, Miller JI, Symbas PN, Hatcher CR Jr: Further Evaluation of the Sutureless, Screw—In Electrode for Cardiac Pacing: Experience with First 300 Implantations. J Thorac Cardiovasc Surg 77:858-862 (Jun), 1979.
125. Drucker MH, Mansour KA, Hatcher CR Jr,Symbas PN: Esophageal Carcinoma: An Agressive Approach. Ann Thorac Surg 28:133-138 (Aug), 1979.
126. Drucker MH, Symbas PN: Right Aortic Arch with Aberrant Left Subclavian Artery:Symptomatic in Adulthood. Am J Surg 139:432-435 (March),1980.
127. Symbas PN, Goldman M, Erbesfeld MH, Vlasis SE: Pulmonary Arteriovenous Fistula, Pulmonary Artery Aneurysm, and Other Vascular Changes of the Lung from Penetrating Trauma. Ann Surg 191:336-340(Mar),1980.
128. Symbas PN, Kelly TF, Vlasis SE, Drucker MFI, Arensberg D: Intimo-intimal Intussusception and other Unusual Manifestations of Aortic Dissection. J Thorac Cardiovasc Surg 79:926-932 (Jun), 1980.
129. Symbas PN, Hatcher CR Jr, Viasis SE: Esophageal Gunshot Injuries. Ann Surg 191:703-707 (Jun), 1980.
130. Finucane BT, Symbas PN, Braswell R: Ligation of Patent Ductus Arteriosus in Premature Neonates: Anesthetic Management. South Med J 74:21-23 (Jan),1981.
131. Majmudar B, Thomas J, Gorelkin L, Symbas PN: Respiratory Obstruction Caused by a Multicentric Granular Cell Tumor of the Laryngotracheobronchial Tree. Hum Pathol 12:183—286 (March), 1981.

132. Wood W, Meier GH, Clements JL, Symbas PN: Function of Fundoplicated Esophageal Segment in Above and Below the Diaphragm Positions. J Surg Res 31:124-127 (Aug), 1981.
133. Stone HH, Symbas PN, Hooper CA: Cefamandole for Prophylaxis Against Infection in Closed Tube Thoracostomy. J Trauma 21:975-977 (Nov),1981.
134. Symbas PN, Hatcher CR Jr, Viasis SE: Bullet Wounds of the Trachea. J Thorac Cardiovasc Surg 83:235-238 (Feb),1982.
135. Wilcox WD, Plauth WIl Jr., Williams WH, Symbas PN: Immediate Postoperative Regurgitant Malfunction of Bjork-Shiley Aortic Valve Due to Interfering Teflon Ventricular Septal Defect Repair: Correction by Rotation of Prosthetic Annulus. Am Heart J 103:148-150 (Jan), 1982.
136. Symbas PN, Viasis SE, Zacharopoulos L, Hatcher CR Jr, Arensberg D: Immediate and Long—Term Outlook for Valve Replacement in Acute Bacterial Endocarditis. Ann Surg 195:721-725 (Jun), 1982.
137. Parmley WW, Hatcher CR Jr, Ewy GA, Frommer PL, Furman 5, Leinbach RC, Redding J, Symbas PN, Weisfeldt ML: Task Force V: Physical Interventions and Adjunctive Therapy. Am J Cardiol 50:409-4 19 (Aug),1982.
138. Symbas PN, Vlasis SE, Zacharopoulos L, Lutz JF: Acute Endocarditis: Surgical Treatment of Aortic Regurgitation and Aortico-Left Ventricular Discontinuity. J Thorac Cardiovasc Surg84:291-296 (Aug),1982.
139. Hoopes IR, Symbas PN, Wenger NK: Cardiac Pacemaker Therapy at Grady Memorial Hospital 1964-1978 (With Patient Follow Up Through 1980),. J Med Assoc GA 71:763-769 (Nov),1982.
140. Symbas PN, Vlasis SE, Zacharopoulos L, Lutz IF: Aortic-Left Ventricular Discontinuity and Aortic Regurgitation from Acute Endocarditis. South Med J 75:1476-1478 (Dec),1982.
141. Symbas PN, Pfaender LM, Drucker MH, Lester JL, Gravanis MB, Zacharopoulos L: Cross—Clamping of the Descending Aorta. J Thorac Cardiovasc Surg 85:300-305 (Feb),1983.

142. Zacharopoulos L and Symbas PN: Internal Temporary Aortic Shunt for Managing Lesions of the Descending Thoracic Aorta. Ann Thorac Surg 35:240-242 (Mar),1983.
143. Symbas PN, Vlasis SE, Hatcher CR Jr: Esophagitis Secondary to Ingestion of Caustic Material. Ann Thorac Surg 36:73-77 (Jul),1983.
144. Greenwald LV, Baisden CE, Symbas PN: Rib Fractures in Coronary Bypass Patients:Radionuclide Detection. Radiology 148:553-554 (Aug), 1983.
145. Baisden CE, Greenwald LV, Symbas PN: Occult Rib Fractures and Brachial Plexus Injury Following Median Sternotomy for Open-Heart Operations. Ann Thorac Surg 38:192-194 (Sept), 1984.
146. Symbas PN, McKeown PP, Hatcher CR Jr, Vlasis SE: Tracheoesophageal Fistula from Carcinoma of the Esophagus. Ann Thorac Surg 38:382-385 (Oct),1984.
147. Symbas PN, Lutz IF, Vlasis SE: Partial Replacement of the Left Ventricular Free Wall with a Dacron Graft: A 14 Year Follow-up. J Thorac Cardiovasc Surg 89:310-313 (Feb), 1985.
148. Symbas PN, McKeown PP, Santora AH, Vlasis SE: Pulmonary Artery Balloon Counterpulsation for Treatment of Jntraoperative Right Ventricular Failure. Ann Thorac Surg39:437-440 (May),1985.
149. Symbas PN, Hunter RM, Vlasis SE, Ansley ID: Infected Descending Aortic Fistula. Ann Thorac Surg 41:647-651 (June), 1986.
150. Symbas PN, Vlasis SE, Hatcher C Jr: Blunt and Penetrating Diaphragmatic Injuries with or without Herniation of Organs into the Chest. Ann Thorac Surg 42:158-162 (Aug),1986.
151. Napoli VM, Symbas PJ, Vroon DH, Symbas PN: Autotransfusion from Experimental Hemothorax: Levels of Coagulation Factors. J Trauma 27:296, 1987.
152. Symbas PN, Vlasis SE, Picone AL and Hatcher CR, Jr: Missiles In The Heart. Ann Thorac Surg, 48:192-4,1989.

153. Symbas PN: Chest Drainage Tubes. SURGICAL CLINICS OF NORTH AMERICA, Philadlephia, W.B. Saunders Co., pp 41-46, Vol. 69, February,1989.
154. Symbas PN, Gott IP: Delayed Sequelae of Thoracic Trauma. SURGICAL CLINICS OF NORTH AMERICA. W. B. Saunders Co. pp 135-142, Vol. 69, No. 1, Feburary,1989.
155. Symbas PN, Pfaender L, Chen H, Gravanis MB: Wrapping and Replacement of Thoracic Aorta: Morphologic and Mechanical Properties. Vasc Surg pp 272-279,1989.
156. Symbas PN, Picone AL, Hatcher CR Jr., Viasis SE: Cardiac Missiles: A Review of the Literature and of the Personal Experience. Ann Surg 211:639-648 (May),1990.
157. Symbas PN, Justicz AG: Spontaneous Rupture of Esophagus: Immediate and Late Results. Am Surg 57:4-7. 1991.
158. Brown PF, Larsen CP, Symbas PN: Management of the Patient with an Asymptomatic Stabbed Chest. South Med J. May, 1991.
159. Symbas PN, Justicz AG, Ricketts RR: Rupture of the Airways from Blunt Trauma:Treatment of Complex Injuries. Ann Thorac Surg 54:177-83, No.1 July 1992.
160. Symbas PN, Justicz AG: Quantum Leap Forward in the Management of Cardiac Trauma: The Pioneering Work of Dwight E. Harken. Ann Thorac Surg. 1993;55-788-9-91.
161. Symbas PN, Justicz, AG, Anderson NA: Immediate and Long term results following repair of aorto-left ventricular discontinuity—A 25 year experience. Cardiovasc Surg (3):337-339, June,1995.
162. Brown WM III, Symbas PN: Pneumocephalus Complicating Routine Thoracotomy:Symptoms, Diagnosis and Management. Ann Thorac Surg 59 (1): 234-6.,January,1995.
163. Symbas PN, Symbas PJ: Missiles in the Cardiovascular System: Chest SurgeryClinics of North America. 7:343-356. May,1997.
164. Blackwell RA, Symbas PN: Delayed Traumatic Aorto-Pulmonary Artery Fistula: The Journal Of Trauma: 44:212-213 1998.

165. Peter J. Symbas, MD, W. Stewart Horsley,MD, Panagiotis N. Symbas,MD: Rupture of the Ascending Aorta, Caused by Blunt Trauma. Ann Thoracic Surgery. 66:113-117,1998.
166. Nikolas P. Symbas,MD, Phillip F. Bongiorno,MD, Panagiotis N. Symbas,MD: Blunt Cardiac Rupture:The Utility of Emergency Department Ultrasound. Ann Thoracic Surgery. 67:1274—1276,1999.
167. Vinod H. Thourani,MD, David V. Feliciano,MD, William A. Cooper,MD, Kevin M.Brady,MD, Andrew B. Adams,BS, Grace S. Rozycki,MD, Panagiotis N. Symbas,MD:Penetrating Cardiac Trauma at an Urban Trauma Center: A 22-Year Perspective. TheAmerican Surgeon. 65:811-818. 1999.
168. Panagiotis N. Symbas, MD, Andrew J. Sherman, MD, Jeffery M. Silver, MD, John D. Symbas, MD, and Jodi J. Lackey, MS: Traumatic Rupture of The Aorta; Immediate or Delayed Repair? Ann of Surg: Vol 235: 796-802, 2002.
169. NP Symbas, PN Symbas: Penetrating cardiac wounds; Evolution of diagnosis, treatment and Results over a 30-year period. Archives of Hellenic Medicine. 30 1-304, 2002.
170. ME Halkos, JD Symbas, PN Symbas: Acute respiratory distress caused by massive thymolipoma: Southern Medical Journal, 97: 1123-1125.
171. ME Halkos, JD Symbas, TM Felner, PN Symbas: Anerysm of the mitral valve: A rare complication of aortic valve endocarditis. Ann Thoracic Surg. 78, 65-66, 2004.
172. JD Symbas, ME Halkos, PN Symbas: Rupture of the innominate artery from blunt trauma; Current options for management. J Card Surg. 20: 455-459, 2005.

Articles, No indexed in Index Medicus

1. Hatcher CR Jr, Logan WD Jr, Symbas PN, Abbott OA: Cardiac Pacemakers: Experience with 135 Patients. Bulletin of Emory University Clinic 5:31-40 (Apr) 1967.
2. Mansour KA, Domey ER, Fleming WH, Logan WD, Khan MZ, Symbas PN, Hatcher CR Jr:Cardiac Pacemakers: Current Status

of Equipment and Implantation Techniques. Staff Physician 18:36-40 (Dec),1972.
3. Symbas PN: Atherosclerotic Coronary Artery Disease: Whom to Refer for Surgery. Consultant 13:117-118 (Feb),1973.
4. Symbas PN: Experimental and Clinical Experience with Autotransfusion. 1st Ann Bentley Autotransfusion Seminar: 1-10 (Sept) 1973.
5. DiOrio DA, Symbas PN, Kourias E: The Effects of Tissue Surfaces and Anticoagulants Upon Blood Component Recovery During Autotransfusion. Bentley Autotransfusion Seminar 2:1—3 (Oct) 1973.
6. Symbas PN: Chest Injuries. Early Diagnosis and Management of Blunt Injury to the Thorax. Ciba-Geigy Limited, Basle (Swizerland): 1-16, 1974.
7. Symbas PN, Hatcher CR Jr: Valve Replacement with Prosthetic Substitutes: A Three-Year Experience with 250 Cases. Panhellenic Surg Congress 485-488,1973.
8. Symbas PN: Surgery of Acquired Valvular Heart Disease. Proc of Rehabilitation Counselor Course: 65-71(Feb) 1976.
9. Symbas PN: Penetrating Injuries of the Chest. Folia traumatologica Geigy. Ciba-Geigy Limited, Basle (Switzerland) 1-16, 1978.
10. Symbas PN, Harlaftis NN: Myocardial Contusion: Diagnostic Value of Cardiac Scanning and Echocardiography. Medical Imaging 3(4):23,4th Quarter, 1978.
11. Symbas PN: Penetrating Wounds of the Heart and Great Vessels. Hellenic Armed Forces Medical Review 13:469-478 (Aug) 1979.
12. Symbas PN: Chest trauma: What injury,What treatment approach? Journal of Cardiovascular Medicine 10: 98(October) 1981.
13. Cheung ED, Ziffer JA, Felner JM, Anagnos D, Symbas PN: Diagnosis and Surgical Treatment of a Primary Lung: Carcinoma Extending into the Left Atrium. Emory Univ. Jrnl of Med. Vol. 5:118-125, No.2 April/June, 1991.

Abstracts

1. Symbas PN, Rosvoll RV, Cho YW :Biochemical and Histological Changes of the Heart Following Interruption of Cardiac Lymph Drainage. Clin Res 14:45, 1966.
2. Symbas PN, Schiant RC: Positive Pressure Ventilation and its Effects on the Cerebral Spinal Fluid, Arterial and Venous Pressures. Clin Res 15:59, 1967.
3. Symbas PN: Coronary Sinus Blood Flow Following Pulmonary Embolization. Clin Res15:224, 1967.
4. Symbas PN, Schiant RC, Gravanis MB, Shepherd R: Effects of Total Interruption of Cardiac Lymph Drainage in Dogs. Clin Res 26:73, 1968.
5. Bonanno JA, Sanders SL, King OW, Blalock GE Jr, Symbas PN: Coronary Vascular Response to Acute Pulmonary Embolization. Clin Res 26:223, 1968.
6. Symbas PN, Ferrier FL, Litman GI, Sybers RG: Pathophysiolgical Sequelae of ExperimentalPapillary Muscle Damage. Clin Res 17:20, 1969.
7. Symbas PN, Levin JL, Ferrier FL, Hudson CB: Auto transfusion. Clin Res 17:34, 1969.
8. Symbas PN, Baldwin BJ, Schiant RC, Sehdeva JS, Hurst JW: Unusual Complication of Bacterial Endocarditis. Circulation 39 and 40 (Supplement 3): 199, 1969.
9. Symbas PN, Galambos J, Underwood F: Experimental Left Atrial Thrombus and Human Atrial Myxoma. Circulation 42 (Supplement 4):l02,1970.
10. Tyras DH, Martin LG, Symbas PN: Myocardial Contusion: Diagnosis by Angiography and Cardiac Scan. Circulation 43 and 44 (Supplement 2):235,1971.
11. Symbas PN, Tyras DH, Hatcher CR Jr, Ortiz V: The Management of Penetrating Cardiac Wounds. Circulation 43 and 44 (Supplement 2): 23 1,1971.

12. Tyras DH, Martin LG, Ware RE, Symbas PN: Myocardial Contusion: Diagnosis by Angiography and Cardiac Scan. Clin Res 20:3 1 1972.
13. Symbas PN, Tyras DH, Ware RE, Baldwin BJ: Alteration of Cardiac Function by Hemodialysis During Experimental Alcohol Intoxication. Circulation 45 and 46 (Supplement 2):227,1 972.
14. Symbas PN, Gravanis MB, Hatcher CR Jr: Myxoma of the Heart:Clinical and Experimental Observations. Chest 64:409, 1973.
15. Symbas PN, DiOrio DA, Tyras DH, Ware RE, Hatcher CR Jr: Delayed Sequelae of Penetrating Cardiac Wounds. Circulation 48 (Supplement 4):5, 1973.
16. Smiley WH ifi, Gilbert CA and Symbas PN: Clinical Evaluation of a Low Profile (Beall) Mitral Valve Prosthesis. Circulation 48 (Supplement 4):219,1973.
17. Hatcher CR Jr, Symbas PN, Jones EL, Mansour KA, Fleming WH: Current Roles of Surgery in the Management of Bacterial Endocarditis. Chest 65:589, 1974.
18. Harlaffis N, Gonzalez AC, Waldo WJ, Symbas PN: Pulmonary Embolism: Correlation of Lung Scanning and Pulmonary Arteriographic Findings. Chest 68:413,1975.
19. Mansour KA, Miller JI, Hatcher CR Jr, Symbas PN: Further Evaluation of the Sutureless, Screw-in Electrode for Cardiac Pacing: Experience with 200 Consecutive Implantations. Chest 72:405, (Sept) 1977.
20. Bloch W, Felner J, Symbas PN, Schlant RC: Ultrasonic Exam of the Porcine Bioprothesis in the Mitral and Aortic Positions in Vitro and in Vivo. Circulation 55 and 56 (Supplement 3):82, (October),1977.
21. Symbas PN, Harlaftis NN: Myocardial Contusion: Diagnostic Value of Cardiac Scanning and Echocardiography. Medical Imaging 3:23 (4th Quarter) 1978.
22. Symbas PN, Hatcher CR Jr, Viasis SE: Immediate and Long Term Outlook for Valve Replacement in Acute Endocarditis. J Cardiovasc Surg 22:458 (Oct) 1981.

23. Symbas PN, Pfaender LM, Chen H, Gravanis MB, Zacharopoulos L: Externally Wrapped or Replaced Thoracic Aorta. Histological and Mechanical Properties. J Cardiovasc Surg 24:3 76 (Jul-Aug) 1983.
24. Symbas PN, Picone AL, Viasis-Hale SE: Cardiac Missiles: A review of the literature and of personal experience. J Cardiovasc Surg 31: (July-Aug) 1990.

Books

1. Symbas PN: TRAUMATIC INJURIES OF THE HEART AND GREAT VESSELS. Springfield, Illinois, Charles C. Thomas, 1972.
2. Symbas PN: TRAUMA TO THE HEART AND GREAT VESSELS, New York, Grune & Stratton, ppl-200, 1979. Also translated into Japanese.
3. Symbas PN: CARDIOTHORACIC TRAUMA, Philadelphia, Pennsylvania, W.B. Saunders Company, 1989.

Chapters in Books

1. Symbas PN, Levin JM, Ferrier FL, Muse AD, Sybers RG: Autotransfusion and Its Effects Upon the Blood Components and the Recipient. In Zuidema GD and Skinner DB (Eds):CURRENT TOPICS IN SURGICAL RESEARCH, New York and London, Academic Press, pp 387-398, Vol 1, 1969.
2. Symbas PN: The Chest Wall and Thoracic Duct. In Martin JD Jr, Haynes CD, Hatcher CR Jr, Smith RB and Stone H}I (Eds): TRAUMA TO THE THORAX AND ABDOMEN, Springfield, Illinois, Charles C. Thomas, pp 149.465, 1969.
3. Stone HH, Symbas PN: The Diaphragm. In Martin ID Jr, Haynes CD, Hatcher CR Jr, Smith RB and Stone H}I (Eds) TRAUMA TO THE THORAX AND ABDOMEN, Springfield, Illinois, Charles C. Thomas, pp 237-245, 1969.
4. Hatcher CR Jr, Logan WD Jr, Symbas PN, Abbott OA: The Use of Valvular Prosthesis for Endocarditis of Aortic Root. In Brewer LA ifi (Ed): PROSTHETIC HEART VALVES, Section lv, Chapter 80, Springfield, Illinois, Charles C. Thomas, pp 706-717, 1969.
5. Symbas PN, Ferrier FL, Sybers RG, Underwood FO: Mitral Valve Function After Experimental Papillary or Left Ventricular Myocardial Infarction. In Ebert PA and Skinner DB (Eds): CURRENT TOPICS IN SURGICAL RESEARCH, New York, Academic Press, Inc., pp 451-461, Vol. 2, 1970.
6. Parmley LF Jr, Symbas PN: Traumatic Heart Disease. fri Hurst JW: THE HEART, New York, McGraw-Hill, pp 1426-1436, Third Edition, 1974.
7. Symbas PN: Rupture of the Aorta from Blunt Trauma. In Edwards WH (Ed): VASCULAR SURGERY, Chap 8, Baltimore, University Press, pp 156-166, 1976.
8. Symbas PN, Hatcher CR Jr: Traumatic Heart Disease. Tn Chung EK (Ed): QUICK REFERENCE TO CARDIOVASCULAR DISEASES, Chap. 15, Philadelphia, Lippincott, pp 208-219, 1977.

9. Symbas PN: Cardiac Trauma. In Levy N (Ed): TRAUMATIC MEDICINE AND SURGERY FOR THE ATTORNEY, Matthew Bender, New York, pp 203-223, Vol. 5, 1977.
10. Symbas PN: Traumatic Heart Disease. In Chung, Edward K. Chap 15, QUICK REFERENCE TO CARDIOVASCULAR DISEASE.Philadelphia, Lippincott, pp 208—219, 1977.
11. Symbas PN, Hatcher CR Jr, Boehm GAW: Acute Penetrating Tracheal Trauma. In Levy N (Ed):TRAUMATIC MEDICINE AND SURGERY FOR THE ATTORNEY, Matthew Bender, New York, pp 255-262, Vol. 5, 1977.
12. Parmley LF Jr, Symbas PN: Traumatic Heart Disease. In Hurst JW, THE HEART, New York, McGraw-Hill, pp 1683-1693, 4th Edition, 1978.
13. Symbas PN: Chest and Heart Injuries. In Schwartz GR, Safar P, Stone JH, Storey PB and Wagner DK (Eds): PRINCIPLES AND PRACTICE OF EMERGENCY MEDICINE, Philadelphia, London, Toronto, W.B. Saunders, pp 653-673, 1978.
14. Symbas PN: Treatment of Thoracic Surgical Aortic Diseases. In Lindsay J Jr, Hurst JW (Eds): THE AORTA, New York, Grune & Stratton, Part VI, pp 359-3 89, 1979.
15. Gray SW, Skandalakis JE, Rowe iS, Symbas PN: Status of Cardiac Surgery: SurgicalEmbryology of the Heart. In Bourne GH: HEARTS AND HEART-LIKE ORGANS.PATHOLOGY AND SURGERY OF THE HEART. New York, Academic Press, pp 239-286, Vol. 3, 1980.
16. Symbas PN: Autotransfusion in Thoracic Trauma. In Hauer JM, Thurer RL and DawsonRB: AUTOTRANSFUSION, New York, ElsevieriNorth Holland, pp 83-92, 1981.
17. Symbas PN: Surgical Treatment of Tracheal-Bronchial Trauma. In Cohn LH: MODERN TECHMCS IN SURGERY, Cardiac/Thoracic Surgery, Installment VI, Futura Publishing Company, Mount Kisco, New York, 46-1 to 46-8, 1981.
18. Symbas PN, Arensberg D: Traumatic Heart Disease. In Hurst JW: THE HEART, New York, McGraw-Hill, pp 1394-1402, 5th Edition, 1981.

19. Symbas PN, Hatcher CR Jr: Techniques of Surgical Treatment of Diseases of the Aorta. In Hurst JW: THE HEART, New York, McGraw-Hill, pp 1913-1922, 5t Edition, 1981.
20. Symbas PN: Thoracic Jnjuries.Invited Commentary by Trinkle 1K and Richardson ID in Carter D and Polk HC Jr: SURGERY I, TRAUMA. Butterworth's International Medical Reviews, Butterworth & Co., Limited, London, 1981.
21. Symbas PN: TRAUMATIC HEART DISEASE, Chicago, Illinois, Year Book, Medical Publishers, 1981.
22. Symbas PN: Blunt and Penetrating Trauma to the Heart. In Glenn WWL, Baue AE, Geha AS, Hammond GL and Lake H: THORACIC AND CARDIOVASCULAR SURGERY, 4th Edition, New York, Appleton-Century-Crofts, pp 1480-1488, 1982.
23. Symbas PN: Traumatic Heart Disease. CURRENT PROBLEMS IN CARDIOLOGY, Vol VII, No. 3, Chicago, Year Book Medical Publishers, Inc. p 4-35, 1982.
24. Symbas PN, Hatcher CR Jr: Traumatic Heart Disease. in Chung EK: QUICK REFERENCE TO CARDIOVASCULAR DISEASE, Philadelphia, J.B. Lippincott, pp 338—348 2nd Edition, 1983.
25. Aletras H, Symbas PN: Hydatid Disease of the Lung. Tn Shields TW: GENERAL THORACIC SURGERY, Philadelphia, Lea & Febiger, pp 645-657, 2nd Edition, 1983.
26. Symbas PN: Penetrating Cardiac Trauma, In Moore EE, Eiseman B, Van Way CW III:CRITICAL DECISIONS IN TRAUMA, St. Louis, C.V. Mosby, pp 158-159, 1984.
27. Symbas PN: Nonepentrating Cardiac Trauma, In Moore EE, Eiseman B, Van Way CW III:CRITICAL DECISIONS iN TRAUMA, St. Louis, C.V. Mosby, pp 160-163, 1984.
28. Symbas PN: Traumatic Pneumothorax. In Edlich RF, Spyker DA: CURRENT EMERGENCY THERAPY, Norwalk, Appleton-Century-Crofis, pp 81-83, 1984.
29. Dedonis J, Schiant RC, Symbas PN: Arterial Air Embolism: An Update. In Hurst JW:CLINICAL ESSAYS ON THE HEART, New York, McGraw-Hill, pp 77-8 1, Vol 3, 1984.

30. Symbas PN, Arensberg D: Traumatic Heart Disease. In Hurst JW, et al: THE HEART, New York, McGraw-Hill, pp 1276-1283, 6th Edition, 1986.
31. Symbas PN, Hatcher CR Jr: Techniques of Surgical Treatment of Disease of the Aorta. In Hurst JW, et al: THE HEART, New York,McGraw-Hill,pp 2043-2052,6th Edition, 1986.
32. Symbas PN, Hatcher CR Jr: Traumatic Heart Disease. In Chung EK: QUICK REFERENCE TO CARDIOVASCULAR DISEASE, Philadelphia, J.B. Lippincott, pp 165-178 3rd Edition, 1985.
33. Symbas PN: Heart Injuries from Blunt Trauma. In Grillo H,et al:INTERNATIONAL TRENDS IN GENERAL THORACIC SURGERY, Philadelphia, W.B. Saunders, Vol. 2, 1985.
34. Symbas PN: Trauma to the Heart and Great Vessels. In Jamieson SW and Shumway NE: CARDIAC SURGERY, Butterworths, Surrey, England, pp 497—508,4th Edition, 1986.
35. Symbas PN: Diverticulum of the Esophagus. In Cameron JL, et al: CURRENT SURGICAL THERAPY—2, Mosby, pp 6-8, 1986.
36. Symbas PN: Chest and Heart Injuries. In Schwartz, et al: PRINCIPLES AND PRACTICE OF EMERGENCY MEDICINE, Philadelphia, W.B. Saunders, pp 1350-1368, Vol. 2, 1986.
37. Symbas PN: Thoracic Trauma. In Peter RM: INTERNATIONAL PRACTICE IN CARDIOTHORACIC SURGERY, Beijing, Science Press (China) and Netherlands, Marinus Nijhoff, Publishers, 1986.
38. Symbas PN, Hatcher CR Jr: Traumatic Heart Disease.In Chung EK: QUICK REFERENCE TO CARDIOVASCULAR DISEASE, Philadelphia, J. B. Lippincott, pp 165-175, 3rdEdjtjOfl 1987.
39. Symbas PN: Cardiovascular Injuries. In Gravanis M: Physiology New York, Mc-Graw Hill 9:261-274, 1987.   I t a l i a n Translation: Fisiopathologia Cardiovasculare. Bruno Magnan i(ed.)New York, Mc-Graw Hill pp 265-278,1987.

40. Symbas PN: Penetrating Injuries to the Heart. In Hurst JW et al: MEDICINE FOR THE PRACTICING PHYSICIAN, Boston, MA, Butterworths, pp:l076, 2' Edition, 1988.
41. Symbas PN: Blunt Injury to the Heart. In Hurst JW et al: MEDICINE FOR THE PRACTICING PHYSICIAN, Boston, MA, Butterworths, pp 1077, Edition, 1988.
42. Symbas PN, Shields, TW: In Shields TW: Diaphragmatic Injuries. GENERAL THORACIC SURGERY, Philadelphia, Lea & Febiger, pp 505-5 12. 3rd edition.1988.
43. Aletras H, Symbas PN: Hydatid Disease of the Lung. In Shields TW: GENERAL THORACIC SURGERY, Philadelphia, Lea & Febiger, pp 83 1-841. 3rd edition. 1988.
44. Symbas PN: The Surgical Treatment of Diseases of the Aorta. In Hurst JW, et al: THE HEART, New York, McGraw-Hill, pp 2224-2232, 7t edition, 1990
45. Symbas PN: Traumatic Heart Disease. In Hurst JW: THE HEART. New York, McGrawHill,pp1375-1381, 7th edition, 1990.
46. Symbas PN: Median Sternotomy or Thoracotomy, In Webb WR: SURGICAL MANAGEMENT OF THE CHEST INJURIES, Mosby Year Book 9,1991.
47. Symbas PN: Traumatic Heart Disease: CURRENT PROBLEMS IN CARDIOLOGY, Vol.XVI No.8:539-582, (August) 1991.
48. Symbas PN: Cardiothoracic Trauma: CURRENT PROBLEMS IN SURGERY. Vol.XVI, No.11:745-797, (November) 1991.
49. Symbas PN: Specific Presentations of Chest Trauma. In Schwartz GR et al: PRINCIPLES AND PRACTICE OF EMERGENCY MEDICiNE 3' ED. Philadelphia, Lea & Febiger, Vol 1: 1047-1064,1992.
50. Symbas PN: Traumatic Heart Disease: IN Toutouzas P,Boudoulas H:CARDIAC DISEASES. Epistimonikes Ekdosis Gregorios Parisinos", Athens Greece 3030-3039,1992.
51. Symbas PN: Traumatic Heart Disease: In Hurst JW, et al: The Heart,8th ed., New York,McGraw-Hill, 2021-2037, 1994.

52. Symbas PN: Traumatic Heart Disease: In Hurst JW: CURRENT THERAPY IN CARDIOVASCULAR DISEASE 4TH ed. St. Louis. Mosby Year Book, 404-406,1994.
53. Skandalakis JE, Gray SW, Symbas PN: The Thoracic And Abdominal Aorta inEmbroyology F SURGEONS Baltimore. Williams and Wilkins, 976-1030,1994 Skandalakis JE, Gray SW, Symbas PN: The Superior And Inferior Venae Cavae inEmbroyology For Surgeons; Baltimore. Williams and Wilkins, 1032-105 1, 1994.
54. Symbas PN, Aletras H: Hydatid Disease of the Lung: In Shields TW: General Thoracic Surgery 4TH ed. Philadelphia Lea & Febiger, 1021—1031,1994.
55. Symbas PN: Diaphragmatic Injuries. In Shields TW: General Thoracic
56. Surgery 4th ed. Philadelphia, Lea & Febiger in press 1994.
57. Symbas PN: Chest Trauma and Emergency Cardiopulmonary Bypass: In Mora CT, Finlayson DC and Rigatti RL: Cardiopulmonary Bypass. New York, Springer Verlag. 1995.
58. Symbas PN: Injury to the Esophagus. Trachea and Bronchus: TRAUMA 3rd ed. Feliciano DV, Moore BE, Mattox KL: Norwalk CT. Appleton and Lange, 375-385, NOV 1995.
59. Symbas PN, Justicz AG: Cardiac Trauma: The CRITICALLY ILL CARDIAC PATIENT. Dantzker D, Kvetan V: Philadelphia, TB Lippincott Company, 22 1-226. 1996.
60. Symbas PN: Penetrating Injuries of the Heart. Medicine for the Practicing Physician; 4TH ed. J Willis Hurst et al. Stamford CT, Appleton and Lange. 1289-1290,1996.
61. Symbas PN: Blunt Injury to the Heart. Medicine for the Practicing Physician 4th ed. J. Willis Hurst et al Appleton and Lange, Stamford Connecticut. 1291, 1996.
62. Symbas PN: Traumatic injuries of the heart and great vessel. The Heart 9th ed. J Willis Hurst et al. Charles C Thomas. Appleton & Lange, Stamford, Connecticut. 1997.
63. Symbas PN, Aletras H: Hydatid disease of the lung: In Shields TW: General Thoracic Surgery 5th ed. Philadephia, Lea & Febiger, 113-1122, 1999.

64. Symbas PN: Diaphragmatic Injuries. In Shields TW: General Thoracic Surgery 5th ed Philadephia, Lea & Febiger, 863-870, 1999.
65. Symbas PN: Traumatic heart diseases. Hurst's The Heart 9th ed. New York, McGraw Hill Medical Publishing Co. 23 19-2326, 1998.
66. Symbas PN, Symbas N:Esophagus:Esophagus and Diaphragm SurgicalApplications: Esophagecotomy through right thoracotomy, Esophagecotomy throughleft thoracotomy, Esophagecotomy without thoracotomy, Benign Tumor Resection. Diaphragm L Resection and Reconstruction. Anatomic Basis of Tumor Surgery 1st ed.William C. Woods,John E. Skandalakis et al. Alexandra Baker. ST Louis, MO. QualityMedical Pub.,271-303, 1999.
67. Symbas PN: Thoracic Trauma: Principles and Practice of Emergency Medicine 4th ed. Schwartz GR, et al. Baltimore, Williams and Wilkins, A. Waverly Co. 300-307, 1999.
68. Symbas PN: Traumatic Heart Disease: Hurst's; THE HEART, 10TH ed., Fuster V., et al. New York, McGraw-Hill Medical Publishing Co. 22 19-2226, 2001
69. Symbas PN: Traumatic Heart Disease: Hurst's; THE HEART, 11TH ed., Furster V., et al New York, McGraw-Hill Medical Publishing Co. 2225-2230, 2004
70. Harlaftis NN, Aletras H, Symbas PN: Hydatid Disease of the Lung: In Shields TW: et a!. GENERAL THEORACIC SURGERY 6th ed. Philadelphia, Lea & Febiger, 1298-1308, 2004
71. Symbas PN: Diaphragmatic Injuries. In Shields TW: GENERAL THEORACIC SURGERY6th ed. Philadelphia, Lea & Febiger, 1006-1014, 2004.